The New Cratylus

The New Cratylus

NOTES ON THE CRAFT OF POETRY

A. D. Hope

MELBOURNE

OXFORD UNIVERSITY PRESS

LONDON   WELLINGTON   NEW YORK

Oxford University Press

OXFORD LONDON GLASGOW
NEW YORK TORONTO MELBOURNE WELLINGTON
IBADAN NAIROBI DAR ES SALAAM CAPE TOWN
KUALA LUMPUR SINGAPORE JAKARTA HONG KONG TOKYO
DELHI BOMBAY CALCUTTA MADRAS KARACHI

First published 1979

NATIONAL LIBRARY OF AUSTRALIA CATALOGUING IN
PUBLICATION DATA

*Hope, Alec Derwent, 1907-
The new cratylus.*

Index
ISBN 0 19 550576 X

*1. Poetry. I. Title.
808.1*

*Published with the assistance of the Literature
Board of the Australia Council.*

TYPESET AND PRINTED IN AUSTRALIA BY BROWN PRIOR ANDERSON PTY LTD
PUBLISHED BY OXFORD UNIVERSITY PRESS, 7 BOWEN CRESCENT, MELBOURNE

Contents

... For he taught them as one having authority, and not as the scribes

MATTHEW 7.29.

Introduction

THIS book has been in my mind for many years and was first planned as an academic treatise when I was a university teacher. Since my retirement from teaching the poet has taken over from the professor and it is presented now as a series of reflections on the craft of poetry which have occurred to me at intervals during half a century of practice, though here and there the professor has contrived to insert some theory.

This has not been a radical change of plan. Many poets I know work by rule of thumb and are innocent of literary theory, but as a poet I have always been keenly interested in the processes that go on in the composition of poems and in the various theories about poetry which have been held in past times and which have proliferated to the danger of poetry itself in the last two centuries. Milton in the seventeenth century, faced with the bewildering variety of theological views, each claiming authority, felt himself obliged to start anew and try to see if a reliable Christian doctrine could not be deduced from scripture alone, which he held to be the inspired word of God. My dilemma in the face of the chaos of theories about poetry in our day, has been much like Milton's, but my confidence in a sure recourse is somewhat less than his was. In these matters there is no sacred and inspired text. But the next best thing is poetry itself. I have tried to suggest the outline of a poetics based mainly on my experience of the making of poems and my direct contact with poems themselves, in several European languages and traditions, poems which readers have generally found themselves agreeing to praise and enjoy. It is no more than an outline and there are gaps in it. The gaps are sometimes left gaping and often they are supplied by guess and surmise, since we still know too little about language and the way it works to put our theories to the test. Beyond these areas of surmise are others still unguessed. This is one of the reasons why I have abandoned the idea of a treatise as beyond our present state of knowledge and beyond my own capacities.

There are two main concerns in the book; one is to explore the *material* of poetry, language, and to consider some new ways of looking at this subject; the other is to describe the way poems seem to come into being and to consider how this may affect our ways of talking about poems, in other words, how a reconsideration of what poets know, and what critics on the whole do not know, may affect critical theory. Interspersed in these two main concerns will be found a certain amount of observation made by the way and not necessarily contributing to the main themes, but relevant to a better understanding of poetry in general.

The original *Cratylus* of Plato is largely a discussion of the essential nature of language and how it works. The essential nature of language and how it works in poetry is my main concern in this book, which is why I have called it *The New Cratylus* rather than *The New Ion*. Plato's *Ion* is about the nature of poetic inspiration and this, while it is a theme of the book, is a secondary concern and depends on the more fundamental theory of language.

I have tried, as far as I can, to write in simple, ordinary English and to avoid the technicalities of criticism and literary theory. Most of such terms are either so vague or metaphorical as to be useless, or have hidden implications which lead those who use them into prejudging what they should be investigating. Whenever I read a critic who uses any sort of literary jargon, I know at once that I am in for muddled thinking and ambiguous conclusions. Whenever I come across a poet who subscribes to such a theory, I am prepared to find the resources of poetry limited and confined and the blind Samson of poetry trudging round and round at the critic's mill.

I should add, I suppose, that I am well aware that in another sense this book is a sort of myth in defence of the sort of poetry I admire and try to practise. The reader should not be deceived by its air of impartial assessment. It is a polemic work and it seeks to discredit bad theories and bad practice of my time. But above all it is a myth in the Platonic sense, an adumbration of the truth in an area of thought still too little explored or understood for a strict demonstration to be possible.

Poets often find such myths a help against too explicit contemporary theories, or simply to promote the emergence of poems. Schiller is said to have believed that the smell of rotten apples in the drawer of his writing desk helped in the inspiration and composition of his poetry. As I dislike Schiller's poems, I shall refrain from the obvious comment. Blake was said to have believed that he took down his poems from dictation by angels. I like Blake's poems but I believe the angels often let him down. From simple cases of useful absurdity like these, it is only a short step to elaborate theories of poetry like those of Alexander Blok, Stéphane Mallarmé, or Edgar Allan Poe, whose chief purpose was not to lay down the law but to provide comfort and reassurance to their authors. I claim no more for mine.

I

Beginnings

IT may well be true that poets are born and not made; but a man born a poet must then make himself one. There are no schools for poets as there are for painters, sculptors, dancers, actors, composers and musical performers. You may be born a poet but you are not born skilled and equipped. Your material is language and at birth you lack even that. The poet's master is himself; a hard master because he is as inept as his pupil.

The beginnings are obscure; they go back at least to the time I was learning to speak, perhaps even to the time when I lay in my cradle making those long strings of crooning and babble, language noises that precede language itself. I can remember learning to speak and my rage when people laughed at my efforts or could not understand my frustration when my tongue would not obey me and I failed to produce the words I could clearly imagine. It was a frustration in later years, and still repeated today when I fail to achieve the shape and tone of an imagined poem. But beyond such conscious effort, lies the period of effortless, pleasurable babble with its repeated rhythms, the first 'making', the first mastery of the most primitive elements of a poem, something which is not yet either language or song but has features of both. I cannot remember that, though I have spent hours listening to babies and recording their progress from one day to another. The deepest roots of poetry are hidden in this lost layer of experience. Even the real beginnings are dark and ambiguous.

We do not really know if a man is born a poet—if he has to be. I have asked others and they cannot remember. Nor can I. Between seven and eight years I recall that I was writing verses of a sort, mostly in ballad metre, the simplest of stanza forms. But I have no memory of when I began, or what prompted it. Nor have I any clue as to whether it was a spontaneous impulse or arose from a child's tendency to imitate any activity that interests him, especially those of grown-ups. People, of course, begin to compose poetry at all sorts of ages and those who do so later in life often confess that the impulse took them by surprise and even beat down all resistance. 'What, me a poet? Don't be ridiculous!' This overmastering urge is often a symptom of the onset of poetry, whether the victim shows any talent for it or not. So perhaps some are born that way, as seems to be the case with some composers and some mathematicians.

Some people seem to be insensitive to everything but the literal, label character of words. Indeed in almost a lifetime of teaching I have found many of my pupils unable to respond at all to poetry, so that I have come to believe that there is a 'word-deafness' comparable to tone-deafness or colour-blindness, an inherent defect of nature, perhaps a gene deficiency of an obscure kind.

However that may be, most children when they are learning to speak, and later when learning to read, seem to enjoy words, play with them, repeat and caress their sounds and the rhythms that link them and find exquisite pleasure in those half-echoes that establish mysterious correspondences between words of something the same sound. I recollect the deep emotion associated with a hymn as I heard the last line:

> Jesus loves me, this I know
> For the Bible tells me so
> Little ones to him belong
> I am weak, but tea is strong!

It was a deep emotion because it helped me to relive the immense pleasure of climbing out of my cot and being allowed to get into bed with my mother—I must have then been four—and to share her early morning cup of tea and slices of thin bread-and-butter with her. The religious associations and implications of the hymn were probably lost on me, but the tune is indelibly associated with something that was (for me) a celebration—*pacè* Freud—a celebration in *words*, of one of my deepest and most central joys. For me still this sense of poetry as a celebration of what is central to human experience is unchanged. The only difference is that I am now aware of a relation, a point of growth, a meaning that I could then not have grasped.

Another hymn I recall that began

> Now the day is over
> Night is drawing nigh

which had a special magic about it and was perhaps my first introduction to that wider diction, that more specifically literary language and syntax than a child is likely to acquire from the conversations of daily life. 'Nigh' for 'near' was a treasure because it was strange, because it gave a peculiar dignity or solemnity to the advent of evening. I began to be aware of possibilities in words beyond their use for social intercourse and the transmitting of information.

Besides hymns there were nursery rhymes. To be bounced up and down on a grown-up's foot or knee to the rhythm of:

> Ride a cock-horse
> To Banbury Cross
> To see a fine lady
> Upon a white horse
>
> Rings on her fingers
> And bells on her toes,
> She shall have music
> Wherever she goes,

was to be introduced to metre both as a physical, and an auditory, experience.

Flashes of memory light up here and there some of this hinterland where the beginnings of poetic interest, poetic awareness and poetic practice took place. As I began to read and write, I recall the pleasure of playing with words, manipulating alphabets cut from cards to put words together, learning quite big words with surprising ease, as if they had some attraction or magic in them. Once I confused 'calvary' with 'cavalry', sitting up in bed in the early morning, and though this was straightened out for me at breakfast when I favoured my parents with the resounding line:

> Their calvary thundered along,

I continued to be enchanted with the mysterious connection of two similar words for such different notions and to have a dim feeling for what Coleridge called the 'inter-inanimation of words'.

For all that, the first step, the moment when I consciously attempted a poem, or unconsciously found I had slipped into it, escapes me. All I am sure of is that two principles or forces were certainly at work: imitation and play—when poets get older they tend to talk about 'tradition' and 'experiment' but these are critical terms and suggest two forces opposed to each other, at least a tug-of-war between two emotional teams. The suggestion is largely true. In later life, in the age I inhabit, the struggle between tradition and breakaway impulse has reached a crisis. But in the beginning, in the first motions of a poet's career, the two cannot be separated. Everything is play. We are practising, learning to use our own muscles as kittens do when they stalk and chase and wrestle together.

Every art begins in this sort of play, but with poetry there is a difference: other child artists are dealing in paint, in clay, in notes of the scale, things outside themselves; the new-hatched poet is dealing in words—words which are inside himself, part of himself, something autonomous and alive, something growing and changing as he grows and changes, something that he is creating and changing as he learns it. This is the kernel of the nut, the centre of the mystery: because from the very start we do not manipulate words as we do paints and brushes; the words come to us from a source we cannot reach; when they come we can dispose them but they, at the same time, are arranging themselves and evoking other words from this hidden source. In a sense they are manipulating us. It is the awareness of this that gives rise to theories of 'inspiration', of possession by the god or the muse. The education of a poet is only partly one of learning to use words; it would perhaps be truer to say that it consists mainly in learning to let the words use him.

My childhood was somewhat solitary. For the early part of it I was taught by my parents: reading, writing and arithmetic from my mother who had been a school-teacher, Latin from my father. He followed the methods by which he had been taught himself. First the declensions of nouns and adjectives, then the conjugations of the verbs, then the other parts of speech and lastly the syntax, words in their natural relations. It was an odd reversal of the way I had learned my first language but I had a good memory, at that time almost a photographic one, and it did not give me too much trouble. I have, of course, never learned to *think* in Latin as I have with other languages, acquired less rigorously and more naturally. My first impulse, faced with a sentence in Latin, is not to read but to construe. Nevertheless, I am grateful to the grammarians' approach. It enabled me to see a language from the inside, to know its anatomy and physiology, the bones and muscles under the skin and how they move and work. When, much later at the age of fourteen or so, I came through to the surface, to the skin, to the bearer of radiance, beauty and vitality, to Latin poetry in the persons of Ovid and Catullus, I had the benefit of two voices in my head, two systems of a music I knew to be parts of a greater and single music. At once I wanted to bring these two voices together, to see if they would fertilize and animate each other. My first published poem was a rendering of Catullus'

Phasellus ille quem videstis, hospites

I must have been about fourteen at the time and my motive was not to translate the Latin poet into English but to see if I could capture in English some of the magical lightness and swiftness of the original. I suspect that, with poets, translation is usually prompted by this desire to find new resources for their art, to rob the hive, rather than to serve their readers. One of my earliest attempts to translate in this sense was finding myself confronted with the deep and solemn music of Virgil's

Tot congesta manu praeruptis oppida saxis,
Fluminaque antiquos subterlabentia muros.

or so it seemed to me then. Wider acquaintance with the range of Virgil's harmonies now makes me wonder why these two lines especially should have leapt out of the page at me with the effect of an epiphany or a revelation. But this is of no consequence. The importance of such contacts is that they are flash-points, moments of attachment, of break-through into another country of the mind and heart, footholds from which one can explore and settle in and become at home there. Henceforth one has direct access; translation, the spurious guide, is paid off and left behind.

It is not necessary for a poet to know other languages than

B

his own, but it is, I believe, a great advantage. The poetry of other languages exerts a constant osmotic pressure on his own; his head is filled with rhythmic patterns which enrich his sense of the untapped resources of his own language. One after another, as an almost unconscious side of my self-education in poetry, I explored and plundered other languages, mostly by my own efforts with a few helping lessons from professional teachers. Always impatient, as soon as I had mastered a few rudiments I pressed on to explore the poetry until I found the 'flash-point' where I felt I had got the essential feel of it. I was always reading ahead of my capacities in vocabulary, grammar and syntax, and always before I could read simple prose with any facility I knew by heart some poems or fragments of poems that had enchanted me. It is, of course, a ridiculous way to attempt a language. I have never mastered any of them properly, but it has served my purpose. Although I have since learned to read a number of them, French, Italian, Spanish, German, Old Icelandic and Russian with reasonable fluency, in the first instance I simply gutted them for their poetry.

There is another advantage in this: one acquires a feeling for language abstracted from its everyday, practical associations and reanimated from its vapid and insipid usage in routine communication and interchange. This is something that it is particularly hard to achieve with one's own language, where the warp and woof of conventional use tends to remove all the overtones of shades and suggestions of meaning on which poetry so much depends. 'Just imagine!' said Anna Akhmatova, on the difficulty of writing lyric poetry, 'A poet works with exactly the same words with which people call one another to drink tea.' If we go straight to poetry in learning another language, we get to the pure essence of language used for poetry, before it has been processed into social cliché or flattened out for us by journalism.

But I am anticipating. Whatever importance other languages may have had for me, English is the medium in which I had to learn to write and my mentors were the English poets, or perhaps I should say the poets who write in English, for some of my early masters were American and one or two were Australian. Now I have described them as 'masters' and 'mentors', and I could speak of 'teachers', but none of these words is quite right for the relationship of a young poet to the models and patterns from which he learns to be a craftsman himself. They do not say: do this! or, avoid that! They do not, in Matthew Arnold's superb phrase 'abide our question'. If they teach, they do it simply by being what they are, an enchantment beyond our reach that we would like to possess. But with a difference. The young poet, however much his verse shows the influence of his admired models, does not wish to imitate them but to emulate them in his own way. Robert Louis Stevenson's 'sedulous ape' or Somerset Maugham's description of how he formed a style by assiduous imitation of Addison may be all very well for writers of prose. A better image for a young poet may well be that of a young tree in a forest, pushing up towards the light and nourished by the composted trunks and leaves of his predecessors rotting and enriching the soil about his roots. Another and perhaps a better image is that of his engaging in a series of love affairs with all the Muses of those predecessors, as Pushkin was said to have drawn inspiration from loving a mistress in Kishinev who had formerly been a bedfellow to Byron.

However that may be, from the time when, about the age of nine or ten, I changed from writing verse for the fun of it to seriously thinking of myself as a poet, I was always discovering and falling in love with one poet after another—and often like John Donne in his prime, with several charmers at once.

Wordsworth, Keats, Shelley, Coleridge, Tennyson, Mrs Browning, Longfellow, Whittier and Lowell stood about my bed, though I cannot recall in what order I met them. I tried Byron but had him removed by parents on the ground that I was too young. I tried Milton but could make nothing of *Paradise Lost*. And of course there was Shakespeare. I remember reading *Titus Andronicus* and *Macbeth* about the age of ten, but as plays. When the poetry dawned on me I hardly know, only that my mind is now soaked with wave after wave of that fertilizing language so that I have only to see a bird flying at dusk to find myself murmuring:

> Light thickens and the crow
> Makes wing to the rooky wood,

or a circle of puff-balls or toadstools in the grass to hear like an enchantment

> The green sour ringlets. . . .
> whereof the ewe not bites.

I never attempt to write a poem of my own, without phrase and fragment of Shakespearean verse starting up like spirits from the grass before my feet. Sometimes they become a positive nuisance, getting in the way and stopping me finding my own words. The same thing has happened with the Authorized Version of the English Bible, which was read to me over and over as a child till its language now forms a permanent substratum of my mind.

Out of this rich compost, towards fourteen, I grew to a new sort of apprenticeship, a deliberate choice of models. Like so many young poets before me, including such unlikely fosterlings as Pope and Cowley, I got my roots into Spenser's *Faerie Queene* and I wrote a long poem in Spenserian stanzas inspired by the incidental tale of Hellenore and the Satyrs and my own fiercely and lyrically awakening sexuality

> The gentle lady loose at random left,
> The greene-woode long did walke, and wander wide
> At wilde adventure, like a forlorne weft,
> Till on a day the *Satyres* her espide
> Straying alone withouten groome or guide;
> Her up they tooke, and with them home her led,
> With them as housewife ever to abide,
> To milk their gotes, and make them cheese and bred,
> And everyone as commune good her handeled.

This is the first time, I remember, that I was aware of the strong connection between sexual feeling—love if you like, they were not divided in my mind at the time, nor indeed since—and the impulse to poetry. It was a feeling that later on led me to remark in a still unpublished poem:

> The poet's, in a certain sense,
> Male organ to the human mind.

A view that I still hold and which demonstrates that my reaction to Spenser was the opposite to that of Cowley in his account of his initiation into poetry:

> I believe I can tell the particular little chance that filled my

head first with such chimes of Verse, as have never since left ringing there: For I remember when I began to read, and to take some pleasure in it, there was wont to lie in my Mother's Parlour (I know not by what accident, for she herself never in her life read any Book but of Devotion) but there was wont to lie Spencer's Works; this I happened to fall upon, and was infinitely delighted with the Stories of the Knights, and Giants, and Monsters, and brave Houses, which I found everywhere there . . . and by degrees with the tinckling of the Rhyme and Dance of the Numbers, so that I think I had read him all over before I was twelve years old, and was thus made a Poet as immediately as a Child is made an Eunuch.

Unfortunately for him, Cowley was right about the sterility of his poetry, whether Spenser was really to blame or not. But I have never ceased to ponder that astonishing simile, since my own experience was so much the other way.

About the same age I acquired a copy of Sampson's edition of William Blake and came on Carey's translation of Dante's *Divine Comedy* and underwent what I can only call an enlargement of the mind, a sense of the metaphysical nature and function of poetry which will take its place later in this book.

My father's library had contained no Australian poets. Apart from a poem or two of Kendall's, I knew none of them in those days except Adam Lindsay Gordon, whose poems I recall giving my mother for her birthday, mainly with a view to reading them myself. But brought up almost completely on English poetry, I went through all the problems of early Australian poets in trying to adapt this tradition to this country. My Romantic mentors had convinced me that poetry should be above all richly poetical, but to achieve this I had to use a vocabulary which would not fit the Australian scene.

> The woods decay, the woods decay and fall
> The vapours weep their burthen to the ground,
> Man comes and tills the field and lies beneath
> And after many a summer dies the swan.

That had the elevation, the tone, what Matthew Arnold had called the 'high seriousness' of great poetry. But put it into equivalent Australian terms

The bush decays, the bush decays and falls
The damp fogs weep their loads upon the ground
Man comes and ploughs the paddock . . .

No, it would not do. 'Ode to a Nightingale' set the pure lyric note in the title itself but 'Ode to a Mopoke', however much I might be moved by the bird's melancholy call on moonlight nights, had something inherently ridiculous about it. When I won a prize for a poem about the Bathurst Plains in an eisteddfod about this time it probably satisfied the set subject by a miracle of dexterity in avoiding any specifically Australian terms.

About this time—fifteen or so—I came under the spell of Browning, who helped me escape from this dilemma by showing me in fact that poetry, and very good poetry, did not have to be 'poetical'. I wrote a great deal of Browningesque blank verse which, if it was poor and diffuse, was at least in 'the ordinary language of men' and got me away from romantic poetic diction. And, as though to balance Browning, two sirens of doubtful reputation, Whitman and Swinburne lured me to their Anthemoessan strand.

Swinburne enchanted me. At fourteen a Latin teacher once caught me scribbling a passionate Swinburnian love-poem under my desk when I was supposed to be construing Caesar's *Gallic War*, and read it to the class amid roars of laughter. No doubt it was rather silly and certainly not based on actual experience. But I learned a great deal from Swinburne's enormous command of English metres and his inexhaustible prosodic invention. And no doubt he helped to balance my taste against Browning's defects of ear and Whitman's 'barbaric yawp'. Whitman shouted, Browning talked in verse, but Swinburne *sang*. And from these exemplars I learned that no poem worth the name must ever be without at least the echo or the suggestion of a singing voice.

Hitherto the young plant had simply grown more or less unreflectingly, taking its nourishment where it could. Now, for the first time I met and began to practise criticism of my own work. Hitherto poetry had been for me a purely private, almost a secret occupation. Now I began to think of it in terms of a reader, and of sharing the craft with others of like mind. My first publications were the translation of Catullus and the prize poem I have mentioned. About this time—I was still in short pants—I met Violet McKee. She was a young painter who had just set up a studio in Bathurst and one afternoon, visiting the house where I boarded, she said: 'I hear you write poetry; would you like to come to tea with me in the studio next week and bring some of your poems?' She was beautiful and self-possessed and friendly, and of course I not only felt the gates to the artists' world and to recognition and companionship open up for the first time, but I fell immediately in love. Next Wednesday came and we sat and talked and drank tea. I read a poem or two and she suggested I leave the pile with her till next week. I walked home several feet above the ground; but next week I came down with a bump. After tea and cakes and talk Vi said: 'I've read your poems and thought about them. I think you have talent but if I were you I would burn all that.' The blow was hard and bitter but I did what she suggested. From then on for many months she set me writing tasks in which she insisted that I write only what I knew about at first hand, always looked firmly at the object and tried to evoke it in the simplest, most direct and economical terms and that I avoid the kind of poem I had been writing, full of personal emotion—indeed, often very second-hand emotion. It was a salutary discipline, and it was the only training in the craft of poetry that I have ever had—indeed almost the only detailed analysis and criticism that I have profited from. It may not have taught me much but it habituated me to think of composition in terms of a single theme, a clean handling of verse, and a connected and clear development. From then on I had at least the minimal equipment to find my own way.

So far I had been quite content to follow the traditional techniques of verse. The university brought me face to face with new experimental modes of poetry, particularly free verse, imagism and symbolism, but while I dabbled in these, they never took hold of me. Mightier and more compelling voices led me another way. I was never seduced, as so many of my poetic generation were, by the modish but essentially trivial fame of T. S. Eliot and Ezra Pound. They could not compete with the master harmonies of Alexander Pope and John Milton whom I was just beginning to explore. And towards the end of my university career, I learned Italian mainly so that I could read Dante in the original. Indeed I have really used Italian very little for other purposes. Once, as I came into an Italian fruit shop in King's Cross where I used to practise my new lingo I heard one of the assistants say to another with a grin: 'Ecco il signore dantesco!' I felt as though I had been honoured.

University study and, later, teaching at last brought me up against the material in which poetry is written and the unfathomable mystery and complexity of language. Critics such as I. A. Richards led me to serious investigation of how language actually works in poetry to produce its effects and the innumerable schools and theories of poetry which kept replacing one another convinced me that none of them had the answer.

All my life I have been trying to get a little closer to that answer. All my life I have been formulating theories, testing them against practice, finding that I must re-formulate, emend or abandon ideas that once seemed complete and self-evident. Now, in old age, I am trying to draw the threads together while I can, to make clear to myself by what fraction I may have drawn a little closer to the answer that always evades us because it presents us always with a new question.

In this, of course, the theory of poetry is no different from the other sciences. Each of them continually advances into an infinite regress of further questions. Nevertheless there is also a continuous growth of positive knowledge. To have added a little to that is all any generation can hope to claim.

One thing, at any rate, that a lifetime of thinking about poetry has convinced me of, is that the starting place for any sound theory is fundamental consideration of the nature of language as the material in which a poet works. When it comes to poetry, I find the linguist, the psychologist and the sociologist—even the philosopher and the historian—helpful but insufficient. That is why I have begun by a brief survey of my own growth and development, the 'sceptical chymist' confronting the *ad hoc* theories of alchemy. The crucible in which this debate is to be decided is the nature of the elements; in our case it is the nature of the Logos, the word.

2

The Material

Socrates: Do you admit a name to be the representation of a thing?

Cratylus: Yes, I do.

Socrates: But do you not allow that some nouns are primitive, and some derived and compound?

Cratylus: Yes, I do.

Socrates: Then if primitive or first nouns are meant to be representations of things, can you think of any better way of framing them than to assimilate them as closely as possible to those objects which they are to represent? or do you prefer the notion of Hermogenes and of many others, who say that names are conventional, and have a meaning to those who have agreed about them, and that it is convention which makes a name right; and whether you abide by our present convention, or make a new and opposite one, according to which you call small great and great skill—that, they would say, makes no difference if only you are agreed. Which of these two notions do you prefer?

Cratylus: Representation by likeness, Socrates, is infinitely better than representation by any chance sign.*

WITH these words Plato raises questions that constitute what is perhaps the first serious discussion of the nature of language in European thought. In the dialogue Socrates and his friends are mainly concerned with the relation of words to the things they denote. Is the relation a natural and essential one, is a name in some way *like* the object it names, or are words purely arbitrary and conventional signs? After some very odd etymologizing and a good deal of plain and fancy dialectic, Socrates concludes in favour of the first supposition. Modern language theories, apart from a few onomatopoeic words that occur in most languages, are in favour

* Plato, *Cratylus* (Jowett's Translation) vol III, p. 98.

of the second. But the debate still goes on and will probably never be satisfactorily resolved.

Language in fact appears to behave in two contradictory ways. In the first place it is plainly an arbitrary code system of sounds or signs which have no necessary likeness to the things and situations they signify. Make the sound combination 'eegle' to an English speaker and he thinks of a large bird of prey, to a German and he thinks of a hedgehog. The association with the concepts 'eagle' and 'igel' in each case is purely conventional. And yet in each case the hearer is right in feeling that the word is 'like' the thing. It has become so by habit and by association. All words are onomatopoeic in this sense—a sense very important for poetry—*they sound like the thing*. There is, so to speak, a natural dogginess about the word 'dog'. We are mistaken, of course, but it is not a mistake likely to impede or distort ordinary communication. For poetry, on the other hand, it is extremely important. Mistake or not, it is what gives language its tone, its colour, its body of feeling, that makes it vivid and differentiates it from a mere code of signals. To anticipate a later stage of this discussion, it is what takes the place of the sensory impact of other arts. A passage for the horn in a musical score is initially simply marks on paper acting as a directive to the performer. The marks are not themselves musical, do not have the peculiar sonorities of horn music. But when we see the series of marks on paper of a line of poetry:

> Triton blowing loud his wreathèd horn

we seem to hear the ghost of sound, so to speak as a quality of the word itself. A different series of marks on paper in a different language will produce the same illusion:

> Et le cerf aux abois tressaille au son du cor.

That it is an illusion we can easily demonstrate by using the same series of sounds or marks on paper in a different context, say Belloc's.

> You have a horn where other brutes have none:
> Rhinoceros, you are an ugly beast.

Now the spectral sound attaching to the word 'horn' is replaced by an equally spectral visual image. This is the way words work: basically as an almost automatic code system of whose operation we are hardly aware, but on the level of awareness, as a continuous ghost-like evocation of images. The primary sense of the word 'imagination' is the process of forming such images. For the most part in ordinary uses of language it occurs quite automatically, but in poetry and various other mental activities we can partly control and direct it. We learn to make voluntary structures of image on the primary structure of code signs, structures not directed to a practical end but to be enjoyed in and for themselves. It is to this second activity, voluntary and pursued mainly for its own sake, that we usually reserve the term 'imagination'.

In order to understand this latter process we must first look more closely at the primary aspects of language considered as code and considered as a process of automatic evocation of images. As the code is the basic aspect of language it should come first.

We have a tendency to think of words as things, particularly since the invention of writing. There is the word on our paper located in space and time like other objects. The tyranny of the eye over the other senses makes us forget that language is primarily something we say and hear. It is not something we see and manipulate, an object, but something we *do*, an action.

It is more or less an accident of course, that vocal noises should form the basis of the code system of language. When I was a boy I once saw two deaf-mutes talking with their hands. What surprised me, because I had just learned the deaf-and dumb alphabet so as to have a 'secret language', was the speed with which they got on; their fingers twinkled through the movements, running them together as we run together the sounds of vocal talk: they were positively chattering. I remember also that they appeared to watch each others' faces rather than the hands, though their hands were held well enough up to be in the field of vision. And those faces were as animated as the hands, working with eyes, eyebrows, lips, sometimes the tongue and gestures of the head and neck, nods and turnings to and fro, smiles, questioning looks and a dozen other expressions which I could not interpret and which came and went, combined with and replaced one another as quickly as the fingers moved—I could have said that they were talking with their faces and their hands together and they possibly were—perhaps using their facial expression as we use intonation and tones of voice to convey fine shades of feeling or meaning. Here was a form of language using gesture alone as the basis of the code, which, as recent studies of animal communication show, is common among many creatures from bees to chimpanzees. But this was no honey-seekers' dance, or group-alerting and group-orienting system. The language my two deaf-mutes were talking was English in all its complexity and sophistication, following all the intricate system of organized habits from which we abstract the formal structure we call English grammar. And there is no doubt that they could have composed English poems in this medium in which nothing *we* could recognize as a spoken word existed, and which, if they were congenital deaf-mutes, neither of the speakers could have had the slightest idea of the sonorities and other audible qualities of speech.

This is a reminder of how purely conventional is the choice of a physical substratum for our code system. The human race could have adopted many others. We could have sung or whistled our thoughts, we could have danced them, or used other complex gesture systems. Indeed we do all these things to some degree. Spoken language is always embedded in and combined with other auxiliary 'language' mediums.

For all that, human language for the most part depends on two code systems, speaking and writing. Both are purely conventional codes, that is to say, they are transmitted from one person to another by a medium so unlike the original thoughts and feelings that it has to be 'translated' for transmission and re-translated on arrival, like a message in Morse code. In speaking, this coding and decoding takes place twice each way. The sender uses his vocal organs to transmit a complicated but organized and orderly series of sound-waves through the air. These waves are collected by the outer ear and passed on as modified vibrations in the tympanic membrane amplified by the bones of the middle ear and the fluid in the cochlea. All these extremely complicated wave notions are then analysed into their simple harmonic parts and these in turn are codified a second time by the auditory nerve, which transmits them in the form of electric impulses to the brain, where they are analysed, sorted and combined and are ultimately 'heard' as sounds, which in turn are decoded as meanings. In writing and reading we complicate the process still further by translating the original sound code into a highly abstract selection of the sound complex now represented by a visual code system; the receiver takes this in through the eye, where the light waves are analysed, sorted and transmitted by a series of code signals in the form of electric impulses to the visual centres of the brain. The brain decodes these messages and we see the visual code, which we then decode in turn into sounds and by a further decoding apprehend as meanings. Moreover, by long habituation in using this incredibly complicated code system, we are, as readers, usually able to restore all the elements of intonation, sonority, stress, pitch and timbre which were not transmitted by code at all, since written or printed language has as a rule no way of indicating these important carriers and modifiers of meaning in spoken communication. It simply records the sounds we call vowels and consonants—sometimes, as in Arabic script, even the vowel signs are omitted. In pictographic systems of writing the ideas themselves are codified and the speech element has to be supplied from habit and memory and then decoded into thought.

It is true, then, that the material in which a poet works is words, but words are anything but simple counters to be consciously arranged in preconceived patterns. We are only able to use language because ninety-nine per cent of the machinery works automatically and, because we are unaware of it, it is beyond our conscious control and directions. If it were not so we would be unable to manipulate the system at all. It would be too complicated for us. Indeed, we still do not understand more than the bare outlines of the physiological and psychological organization involved and the leap from code to thought or feeling, from a physiological activity to a mental experience, is a completely blank spot in our understanding of the process. We know only that it happens.

People who use language professionally, poets and literary theorists, are usually aware that language is a very complex system. But they are often ignorant that its mode of operation is even more complex and this leads to ideas about language which are false or over-simple. Perhaps the commonest cause of error is that of thinking of language as

'material'. We think of its components, words, as things to
be manipulated. But a word is not an object, it is an activity;
it expresses thought or feeling, or it arouses thought or feel-
ing. Thinking and feeling are ways in which we behave. We
become the victims of idiom when, like so many philoso-
phers, we talk of thoughts or images being 'in the mind'. The
images of poetry are not objects, but part of the activity of
'imagining'. The moment we forget this fundamental fact we
go astray in forming theories of poetry. Some of these false
theories will be discussed in a later chapter, but we can men-
tion here the common treatment of poetry as a sort of paint-
ing or depiction, which, starting with Aristotle, has given
rise to various 'imitation' theories of literature.

The activity which we call speaking and writing is com-
monly thought of as primarily a matter of communication,
and it is certainly that among other things. When it takes the
form of poetry, communication of information may not be
a particularly important end. Much more important as a
rule are elements akin to music, dancing and play, of which
we shall have more to say later. But we are so apt to think of
language in terms of communication of information that we
tend to overlook two other functions of words, very im-
portant for poetry, which I call 'perception' and 'conversa-
tion'.

We do not ordinarily think of speech as a means of percep-
tion, except as an activity designed to get the hearer to per-
ceive what we are saying. But in fact it is a means to perceiv-
ing what is going on in other minds. Human senses are very
much dominated by the sense of sight. Hearing with us is in
almost every respect inferior to vision, both in its range and
accuracy in discerning what is going on in the world around
us. Other animal species have reversed this position. Bats
can 'see' with their ears better than with their eyes. Pit-vipers
and some other reptiles use heat-sensitive organs as we use
our eyes. But in one respect hearing is superior to vision and
that is in conveying information of what is going on in our
minds, both in the way of thought and of feeling. This has a
detail, a refinement and a delicacy far beyond the facial and
bodily indications we transmit through the visual sense and
is for the most part made possible by human speech. No
mime or dance can match the resources of a poem or the

dialogue of a play.

We are all aware of this. What we are not so well aware of is that we use language not only to send out signals but also to provoke echoes and replies, in very much the way that bats, and possibly dolphins, use their own voices for echo-sounding, the general principle on which radar is based. When language is used successfully in this way, what ensues is a *conversation*. A conversation is much more than communication, though it is based on two-way communication. The parties to a conversation are not necessarily exchanging information, though a good deal of information may be in fact exchanged. What they are primarily engaged in exchanging is awareness of each other's minds. Conversation, unlike argument, instruction, practical exchange of information, narrative and description, though it may include some or all of these purposive uses of language, is quite clearly distinguished from them by the fact that it has no purpose. It is not directed to any end. Its mode is contemplation, discovery and recognition.

There is a sense in which a poem is a kind of conversation with an unknown person, with a mind which is imagined and projected into space by the poem itself, like the pollen grains of wind-inseminated plants scattered out to find their opposite numbers. On this theory of elective affinities, the poem becomes the source of an endless series of conversations in the sense in which I have just used the word. The participants rarely meet. In most cases one of them is already dead, and yet the conversation takes place. A short while ago, through a third party, I received this comment on some of my own poems which brings out exactly what I mean by a poem as the essential part of an ideal conversation:

> Whatever journeys I have taken to the dark places inside myself, he has been there already, and has been able to describe them on his return in the simplest and most lucid phrases, the kind I always look for but can never find.

This use of language as an instrument or means of perception suggests another way in which the elaborate code-systems already described in rough outline, seem to work. In the older and more automatic systems such as those of sight and hearing we no doubt have in infancy to learn to recog-

ize signals of the code and to interpret and translate them
into sensory experiences. But it happens without any con-
scious effort on our part. To most of us it seems that when
we look or hear we have direct perception of the world out-
side us. In the younger code-systems such as that of language
we are conscious of having first to perceive the code signals
through ear or eye and then to interpret them. We naturally
contrast the vivid sensory perceptions of sound, colour and
shape, with the apparently less direct impression of visual
and auditory experience we obtain through words and think
of this as 'indirect perception'. What we overlook is that
language may give us direct perception of our mental experi-
ence of colours and sounds. Memory or imagination may not
be able to give us the actual sensory impressions of these
things as the eye and ear convey them, but when transmitted
through language they do give us the actual experience of
remembering or imagining such things. As we have seen,
there is no such thing as 'immediate perception'. The illu-
sion of it only arises in the older senses because we are un-
aware of the complex coding and decoding necessary for
seeing and learning, and these older senses are not totally
automatic; if they were, they could not adjust themselves to
new or variable situations.

We are continually enlarging the range of things we can
perceive directly instead of consciously perceiving the code
and subsequently inferring what is to be perceived. A simple
example of this is the perception of one shape in terms of
another, or using that other as the carrier of our code. I see
a circular plate lying on a table a few feet away from me.
What actually falls on my retina is not a circle but an ellipse
and with a little practice, I can learn to see it as an elliptical
shape, though the effect of seeing it as a true circle is so
strong that even then, experimenters tell me, I see it as an
ellipse intermediate between the circle and the actual oval
that falls on the retina. It is usual to talk as though we
really saw an ellipse and had learned to interpret it as a
circle, and no doubt this is what we once had to do. But now
the process is, so to speak, short-circuited: we actually see a
circle and the ellipse simply becomes a means, a code signal
like the electric impulses in the optic nerve, of which we are
unaware. An original inference has become a direct or im-

mediate perception. Any one who wants to become a painter has to learn painfully to perceive the code signals and represent them and not what they convey, what he ordinarily perceives. Otherwise, for example, he will show us shapes without allowance for perspective. By not distorting them he will show them distorted.

This extension of the range of direct perception by learning to see what was at first only inferred applies to all the senses and to all combinations of the senses. It is what underlies Gestalt psychology: the *Gestalten*, the whole images by means of which we see and interpret details and even fill in details not actually there, are part of an inherited or a learned code. The codes may be of many and of mixed kinds. There is a difference for example, between codes which are of the same kind as the things perceived and those which are not. The code which allows us to see the visible world as it is, to use the effects of perspective as a means of perceiving the distance of objects, is itself a visual perception. So is the process by which stereoscopic vision allows us to use two flat pictures of the same object seen from slightly different angles as a means of seeing it *in the round*, three dimensionally. But other codes are conventional. We can perceive other people's joy, or grief, or fear by looking at the muscular changes in their faces. Muscular changes form a code which is not in itself emotional. As Darwin showed, we may easily be mistaken about a chimpanzee's emotions though he uses a similar muscular code.

Another example, and an interesting one, is reading. A glance at a poem written in an unknown script is enough to remind us that the marks on paper do not in themselves convey sounds. We have to learn by a slow process to associate writing with the sounds of words. A child learning to read by one of the alphabetic methods has at first to interpret each letter and then infer the sound and meaning of the whole. Later this process short-circuits itself. He looks and sees a word, and from putting word to word in the same way he learns to look and see whole sentences. The marks on paper become a means of seeing sounds directly, as the ellipse on the retina becomes a means of seeing a circle. Interpretation has passed over into direct perception.

c

This example is worth thinking about because it leads into my main argument. When a practised reader looks at words on paper he perceives sounds and not marks on paper which he interprets as sounds. But of course he *hears* no sound, any more than a musician does in reading a musical score. What he perceives is not actual sounds but their 'ghosts'. He perceives what occurs in our minds when we *think* of the word. It is what we call a mental image of a sound. The musician reading a score perceives the mental image of a sonata. The score itself may be compared with a gramophone record. A gramophone record contains a code in the form of irregularities in the groove which can reproduce actual sounds. The musical score contains a similar code which can be used to perceive the mental image of the music played by the gramophone.

Up to this point I have been suggesting two things about perception of the external world. The first is that even what we seem to perceive directly is always mediated, it is always conveyed to us in some sort of code which is translated into sensory terms. There is no such thing as unmediated perception. The second thing is the idea that we can and do constantly extend the range of what we perceive by learning to substitute sensory experience for an original inference from another sensory experience which is now treated as a code and more or less ignored. In this way parts of the world inaccessible to knowledge except in roundabout ways become accessible to direct inspection.

One part of the world usually assumed to be inaccessible in this way is the minds of other people. Each of us is supposed to have an inner mental world of consciousness whose thoughts and feelings are not only as inviolable as our digestive processes, but strictly incommunicable even when we would like to lay our minds open to someone else. The best we can do is to behave in ways that will give other people an idea, by analogy of what they too think and feel, of what is going on in our private world. One of these ways is speech and as speech consists of an artificial system of sound symbolism—a more or less abstract code—the best we can do with it is to communicate code-signals which are a more or less crude indication of possible states of mind. But no one can possibly inspect any one else's state of mind. There is no possible way of direct perception of another person's consciousness. This, as I say, is a very common view of the matter. The novelist Patrick White uses a quotation from Olive Schreiner as an epigraph to *The Aunt's Story*, a quotation which expresses the view very well:

> She thought of the narrowness of the limits within which the human soul may speak and be understood by its nearest of mental kin, of how soon it reaches that solitary land of the individual experience, in which no fellow foot-fall is ever heard.

My contention is that this common view of the solipsist consciousness is false, or at least greatly exaggerated. Gesture, movements, expression and vocal cries can form a code which, at first interpreted inferentially, soon becomes a means of direct perception. At first we see the smile, soon we perceive the joy, the welcome, the amusement or the derision which the smile acts as a code-signal for. But language provides us with a code which in the same way enables us to follow and then perceive the inner life of other peoples' minds with vastly more delicacy and precision. It may be compared in this respect to visual compared with auditory perception. As I said before, some bats apparently 'see' with their ears, that is to say they perceive shapes, masses, motions and relations of bodies by sound, just as our eyes do by light. But human hearing is a comparatively limited instrument for such purposes. It can detect distance and direction roughly and the size of bodies producing or reflecting sounds even more roughly, but what people say tells us infinitely more about them than other ways in which they behave. It is a code so delicate, so flexible in its means that any two people who live much together soon learn to ignore the code as the practised reader ignores the letter signs on the paper; they come readily to a highly expert ability to perceive each other's mental life directly—though of course what they perceive is only the part of that mental life which is made available. Speech and gesture can be refrained from, controlled and directed. A language thus represents an inheritance of common social experience without which the code could never be more than a code. Its possibilities as a means of perception, of stored consciousness, depend on a common civilization which will ensure that the code can be automatically translated. For unless the processes are automatic the code-signals will be all one can perceive. A language which constantly varied and changed its alphabet or its spelling would keep readers at the level of inferential reception; they would constantly be perceiving the letters, whereas perception of words as sounds requires us to forget the letters.

And this brings me at last to poetry. If my theory is correct a poem is a state of mind extended and developed in time, a mental experience conveyed in a code. It need not be a communication in any simple sense; it is a creation, from the material provided by language, of a new mental state or experience. It may focus on the external world, as in a story or a description; it may equally well focus on the internal world, as in a lyric or a meditative poem. It may be personal or it may be impersonal. But its material is always mental experience. Its effect is to create states of consciousness which can be directly perceived. There is, of course, nothing perverse in applying this to a sonnet by Shakespeare. Shakespeare is dead but his conscious mind is coded in such a way that we can still directly perceive it as we can perceive the voice of Caruso from a gramophone record or the explosion of a supernova that happened millions of light-years ago in a distant part of the universe. In fact the mental experience which was once a process of a living mind has come to life again as I read the sonnet. It has become a process of mind; while I read, recall or recite, however, there is not recreation of the original in the sense in which the gramophone record reproduces the voice of the singer. My translation of it is coloured by my world of experience in a way that will be considered in the next chapter. The poem takes on dimensions and shades of interpretation different from those evoked in the original mind. The life it leads in me is parasitic. It is like the figures of Helen and Alexander the Great to which Faustus gave a temporary body and life, a demonic life under the control of the magician and not of their own personalities, wills and desires. It is, moreover, something which, however much I lend it animation, I am myself incapable of producing. Only Shakespeare could do that and he has long since broken his staff and buried it and deeper than did ever plummet sound has he drowned his book.

3

Dream Work

IT was a poet, Paul Valéry, who drew attention to another aspect of words. He called them: 'Ces merveilleux petits songes brefs', ('these wonderful little short dreams'). If someone utters the word 'horse', it is as though I had a short waking dream of the animal in question. And if I read the word in a context of other words, such as 'And I looked, and behold, a pale horse: and his name that sat on him was death, and hell followed with him', it is enough to recall the four horsemen of the Apocalypse as a more detached momentary dream. Our mental life, in so far as it consists of thoughts and feelings, has very much the character of controlled dreaming. For most of our waking life what we are 'dreaming' about is the world around us, we are dealing with its demands in a practical way. Our dream-work is engaged and controlled by our environment and directed by our aims and the feelings attached to those aims. But in literature, especially in poetry, whether we are composing it or reading or hearing it, we are in a state much closer to that of the dreams of sleep. This is, in fact, the other side of the material of poetry of which in the last chapter we considered the mechanism. As a state of mind, experienced from the inside, as a conscious activity, this mechanism of coding and decoding is a sort of controlled waking dreaming. What distinguishes it from ordinary dreaming is the fact that we are awake, aware of our surroundings and aware, too, that we are composing writing, or on the other hand, hearing or reading. What links it with the dreaming we do when we are asleep is that there is always an element in poetry that comes to us unbidden, no matter how consciously and deliberately we compose. Poetry is partly making and partly finding; it is very definitely a craft, but the skills are not entirely under the conscious control of the craftsman. In our education for the practical activities of life, we learn with more or less success to use words in solving problems, designing means to achieve our ends, in communicating our ideas to others and so on. A poet has to learn to use words in a rather different way because they are not directed to some purpose outside the poem. The poem is an end in itself and until it emerges and its shape is visible he does not know exactly what he is aiming at. At first his task consists in helping the poem to make itself.

Another element that distinguishes the use of language in poetry from its other uses in the practical world is that of play. Play is also a frequent element in dream work. Most of my life I have taken a great interest in my own dreams and have also taken trouble to record and study them. In particular I have been interested in what I call 'Kublai Khan dreams', dreams in which I compose poems, write plays in verse, construct novels and write sections of them, give lectures and propose educational theories. They fade rapidly on waking but I often manage to capture fragments and write them down. I say that I dream that I am composing but this is not usually the case. My impression is that those parts of the team engaged in the composition of poems, take advantage of the fact that the part of me that says 'I' is temporarily absent, asleep. They, so to speak, take over the studio and play at composition. They sometimes produce some amusing ideas or some brilliant phrases, but their efforts have only a specious coherence, the details are often not filled in and their more ambitious efforts, such as the elaboration of a scientific theory or a connected plot, turn out on waking to be a mere mock-up of what was intended. Above all, there is a feeling of playing at composition, of acting a sort of charade, like children 'dressing up'.

For example I once woke from a dream in which I was reading a book by Coleridge in which he quoted some seventeenth century author

> . . . that, fire being the noblest of the elements, to burn even a temple was no sacrilege.

That I think is well enough for dream work, but Coleridge was a mere lay figure, and what I could recall of the rest of the book on waking was incoherent and bore no resemblance to Coleridge either in style or his usual range of interests and ideas.

A good many of these dreams are marked by an exuberant and obviously sportive playing with words. Here is a note of one I made about five years ago:

> I woke from a dream in which I was in company where a poet whom I did not know was complaining about having to live in modern society—just why was not made clear. Someone remarked that he should meet the poet Rodney Hall who, he said, had just come back to Australia after several years living in the womb of Rima. In the dream I am aware that this is a compound pun combining the Russian name for Rome (*Rima*) with the Italian word (Rima) for rhyme (or verse) and also a reference to Epstein's well-known statue of Rima, the heroine half-bird and half-woman of W. H. Hudson's romance *Green Mansions*.

I recollect that the dream workers took pains to make this clear and seemed very pleased with themselves. But the three references actually have no connection that makes sense and *Rim*, not *Rima*, is actually the Russian word for Rome. Nor has any of it anything to do as far as I can see with my friend Rodney Hall.

In another dream a year or so earlier in Noumea I seemed to be having an argument or discussion with someone to whom I quoted Mallarmé's

> Un coup de dès jamais n'abolira le hasard

To which my interlocutor instantly replied:

> Un chien qui manque de dents jamais ne pensera.

In the dream this seemed to be a most profound and witty comment on the first line and, in addition, to imply a whole theory of animal intelligence. Neither of these impressions survived a waking scrutiny.

A similar false sense of relevance occurred, I remember, in a dream in which I was, as I supposed, working at the conclusion of a poem I had started the night before. I actually finished this dream work after I came to the surface and was satisfied that the final two lines were an integral part of the nearly completed poem and quite successful in themselves. I wrote them down and went back to sleep. In the morning I found that I had written:

The rock of thought, not yet furred with flesh
Nor that flesh luminous with renascent light.

This was in no way relevant to my poem in progress nor did it seem to mean anything much in itself.

For all that the two lines, while they seem to make no sense, do have an evocative quality. They seem to be reaching towards a meaning that lies just beyond the range of apprehension. They have, as it were, the overtones and emotive suggestions which are characteristic of true poems. They produce an effect which could neither be foreseen nor planned in advance and which no recipe or craft-skill could be invoked to produce.

The three examples quoted from my own dreams all have in common this quality of playful invention, the suggestion of unexpected verbal felicity which a genuine poem always displays, but they also have in common that lack of inner structure, connection and 'point' that a genuine poem must also have. A surrealist poet would recognize them as typical of his so-called poems except that they are in metre, something that his subconscious mind has apparently never been able to master. It is, in fact, the combination of the tedious shuffle of so-called free-verse with the incoherent vomit of that uncontrolled subconscious,

la bouche
Sépulcrale d'égout bavant boue et rubis

that makes most surrealist verse so unpleasant in spite of the often brilliant and sometimes beautiful images that sprinkle it, the rubies dotting the formless mud. The difference between the dream poems from which I have quoted, or, say, Coleridge's 'Kublai Khan' and surrealist verse, is that the former do have a superficial order and coherence, the latter have none. But essentially they are productions of the same kind. They demonstrate what happens when the alert and aware organization of the craftsman is removed.

There are, in fact, two operations necessary in the composition of poetry: one is what I call the dream work; the other, the intellectual ordering and supervision I call the craft work. Dryden has beautifully described the two processes in his dedication of his play *The Rival Ladies* to the Earl of Orrery:

My Lord, this worthless present was designed you long before it was a play; when it was a confused mass of thoughts, tumbling over one another in the dark; when the fancy was yet in its first work, moving the sleeping images of things towards the light, there to be distinguished, and then either chosen or rejected by the judgment.

Dryden speaks as though the dream work preceded the craft-work but they commonly go on together and often their interaction is very complex. This is a subject to which I mean to return in a later chapter.

I deliberately chose from my notes on my dream compositions examples in which craft work was clearly enough defective to show the dream work separately. In general the dream workers are unable to handle structure, but occasionally they can do much better than the samples just given. Some time in 1969 I had a dream in which I was attending the first performance of a newly discovered comedy by Menander—I have never read anything by Menander and know very little about him. The play was presented in an English translation. I was sitting in the front row of a small theatre and facing the empty stage when a man came onto the stage dressed as a Greek farmer—so I imagined—wearing sandals and a simple dress of sackcloth which came to his knees and was gathered in at the waist with a rope or belt. He was wearing a wide-brimmed traveller's hat and carried a traveller's staff, and it was clear that he was to speak the prologue— about twenty lines in all. Its theme was a journey which the rustic felt impelled to make in order to see someone called Alexander, because somebody, he felt, should protest at the ruler's policy, which threatened to ruin the country. It set the scene for a plot which was vaguely suggested. I woke up at the end of the countryman's speech with the whole of it clearly in mind and at once put on the light and began to write it down. But as usual the text began to fade and I only managed to capture odd lines:

> It may seem strange to many that I
> A simple ploughman should be setting out
> On such an improbable journey,
> But somebody has to do something.
> . . .
> I know not what I shall do

Nor how I shall greet him
. . .
It will come to me when I get there
As happens to everyone . . .
. . .
. . .
My hand against Alexander.

I am sorry that I was not able to get the whole thing down because, as I first recollected it, it was coherent, sensible and in style very like the sort of translation of ancient Greek play conversation that one is accustomed to read. On a later occasion when I was actually trying to read the *Alkestis* of Euripides in the original Greek with marked lack of success, I gave up, turned off the light and went to sleep. Some time in the night I woke from a dream in which I was reading the play with some ease and the help of a verse translation. I recalled the speech of the leader of the chorus (or possibly the god Apollo) to a member of Admetus' household who seemed to be a soothsayer or prophet—there is no such character in Euripides' play, of course—the speaker was addressing him with scornful irony:

Truly then thou must be the happiest of men,
Who hast the praise of the dead,
The esteem of the living,
The house of the god [to live in],
    and a fee!

The verse of these examples is loose and irregular but the dream workers, unlike the subconscious, seem able to handle various regular metres and even to invent metrical forms. For example, not long ago I had a dream of composing a poem in hexameters, a metre I rarely attempt and never successfully. I woke retaining only the last line:

But isn't cold catachresis what we are actually
                                    seeking?

A nonsense question since neither I nor the dream team had the slightest idea what 'catachresis' might be, except that it was some kind of technical literary term.

Perhaps the dream workers' most ambitious venture in metrical invention among those I remember was 'The Pilgrim Song'. In the dream in which it occurred I was visiting a city in eastern Europe on the occasion of an annual student 'rag' which took place in the city square. The Pilgrim Song, I understood, was a traditional form with a refrain always repeated, to which each year the university students composed satirical stanzas. It was sung to a very charming tune in a minor key and was accompanied by a whirling and stamping dance. Out of this elaborate scenario I managed to retain several of the dozens of stanzas as well as the refrain:

> As I wandered out
> Intending for to play
> The moon shone about
> On the Pilgrims Way.
> Whom should I meet
> And what should I see?
> I cannot tell you yet,
> A-coming after me.
> She was not like a woman,
> A lion, a leaf, a ball
> Nothing like that,
> No!
> Nothing like that at all.
> . . .
> A poor wandering scholar
> Raggèd all behind,
> Poxed all before,
> Almost out of his mind.
> . . .
> . . .
> . . .
> . . .
> She was not like a woman
> A lion, a leaf, a ball
> Nothing like that,
> No!
> Nothing like that at all.

The difference between actual dream composition of this sort and that which takes place in waking life, is that when awake one is aware of the contribution and participation of the dream team going on just below the surface, but also of a controlling and directing co-ordinator, choosing and rejecting, substituting and trying different alternatives, checking meanings and filling gaps and above all, supervising the growth and direction of the poem as a whole. Real dream poems tend like dreams in general to change scene, direction and sequence of thought and feeling in a desultory and arbitrary way. One suspects from the two fragments of 'Kublai Khan' which Coleridge managed to salvage from the visitor from Porlock's intrusion, that it, too, had no great cohesion. One would never guess from the fragments themselves that they were connected in any way or part of the one poem. The dream workers on the whole give the impression of *playing* at poetry. Indeed, this is what chiefly distinguishes their efforts from the waking mind's experience of putting a poem together: a serious intention to produce something whole, connected and coherent.

I can perhaps add to these reflections by an example of the stages of composition of an actual poem consciously composed and, what is rare with me, clearly recalled. One tends to compose in an intense, half-hypnotic, half-dream-like state and to forget very quickly the processes that led up to it, once the final draft of the poem is complete. I have no doubt forgotten a great deal about the details of the composition of this poem but I did keep the drafts and I do recall the main stages and the main ingredients and processes that led up to it. The poem is called 'As well as they can,' and was written fairly easily over two or three days in 1969. But in fact the poem had been growing very slowly long before that.

What started it going was not a phrase or a suggestion pushed up from the dream workers, the commonest germinal point of poems for me, but one that is almost as common, a spark struck by the way in the course of my reading. Some time in 1940 I came across some poems by Henri Michaux and one line seemed to leap out of its context and, as it were, claim a context in my own mind in some possible, but as yet unconceived poem:

Le poisson pêché pense à l'eau tant qu'il le peut.*

Within seconds the image from the French poem took root and began to grow more roots as an illustration of other situations, an exile, a poet struggling to keep his mind on the world of his poem in all the clatter and distraction of daily living, a lover with the misery of a lost mistress, the survivor of a marriage or a close friendship when one partner has

* The fish caught by the hook thinks of the water as well as it can.

died. All this was very faintly adumbrated, very tentative—a sense of *that sort of thing* rather than any definite outline or topic, a feeling that could best be expressed by: there is a poem there somewhere if I can discover it. And with it that curious sense of alert excitement which so often heralds the onset of a poem.

At the same time as the image was taking root and beginning to proliferate, it began to reach out, draw on memory by a sort of chemical combination with personal experiences to something, bred from each, but new in itself. I had a very sudden and vivid memory from my boyhood when I had been sent to show a visiting fisherman the best pools for trout in the part of the river that ran at the bottom of my parents' garden. I saw the cast, the trout rising to the fly from the deep still pool, the playing of the fish till it was drawn into the shallows and netted to the grassy bank, where my companion wrenched the hook from the torn jaw of the creature, holding it down with boot and hand. The fish slipped and escaped into the coarse sand near the pool and was recaptured, all its side covered with dirt and, what horrified me most, grit embedded in its eye. It was then put in the fishing basket, where it continued to thresh and flap about till it died. This vivid, cruel but exciting personal experience fused with the line of the poem and with my memory of swimming in the same reach of the river, head under water with a sense of the deep, cool, tranquil life of the fish down there. I made a few scrappy notes and attempts at a first stanza, but the poem evaded me and I abandoned it for another eleven years, though I came back to the idea every so often. I got no further. Yet I was haunted by the feeling that the poem was *down there* like the fish under the bank in the pool and that the dream work was going on.

In the meantime, about four years after the first strike, I was working out another poem 'Dragon Music', in which I used the idea of the fish leaping from the water to die on the bank as an image of passionate love. It was partly a deliberate borrowing from the still inchoate earlier poem and partly it seemed to offer itself as a solution to my problem of how to bring the poem both to a conclusion and a climax. What I borrowed, however, seems to have reacted on the material of the earlier poem and helped to give it direction

among the vague choices that had partly presented them-
selves. Yet the final form of poem still evaded me and it re-
fused to 'crystallize'. Then about 1951, during another
return to the subject, quite suddenly it began to come
through. First in the form of definite structure; it was as
though I 'saw' the poem in rough outline. The subterranean
dream work of this long gestation had reduced it to a poem
of three sections, each paralleling the others, the fish, the
poet, the lover. With this came a first title: 'Fish out of
Water', and the metre iambic pentameter, each of them
'offered' rather than deliberately chosen. The first rough
draft lay on the page:

> As well as it can the fish upon the bank
> Fighting the air, threshing the . . .
> Its jaw ripped by the hook, its tender eyes
> Peppered and punctured by the . . . grit
> Thinks of the bland water of the pool
>
> As well as he can the poet in his . . .
> Hooked by his hands and . . .
> And wills itself into its native . . .
> Keeps his mind on the . . .
> And gasps between the throes of . . . and . . .
> Words that he hopes . . .
> By some impossible magic to regain
> The liquid deeps, the cool deep grots of song
>
> As well as it can my heart in the rough air . . .

After a period of perfectly conscious and deliberate experi-
menting with this not very coherent material something
happened that I can best describe as the poem choosing its
stanza form and at once it began to pull together and shrink
into a definite shape. I have often observed that one of the
functions of a definite metre and stanza is to help select and
order the thoughts and the various alternative verbal sug-
gestions; rhyme usually has the same function. Mallarmé
speaks of a poem crystallizing on the twig of metre, an image
borrowed from Stendhal's *de l'Amour*. But a stanza form
often operates in the same way. It is another argument in
favour of regular forms in poetry.

The next draft (about 1967) looked like this:

> As well as it can the hooked fish as it dies
> Gasping for life, threshing in terror and pain,

Its torn mouth parched, grit in its delicate eyes,
    Thinks water thoughts again
As well as he can the poet in his rage

. . .

. . . age
    Taps the pure source of song
As well as I can my heart in the bleak air,
The empty days, the waste nights since you went,
Recalls your touch, your voice your silences that were
    Its native element.

From this point on the dream work subsided and the further work on the poem was one of conscious trial and substitution of alternative words and ideas. I was still at a loss for a satisfactory image for the poet and all my efforts tended to be faintly comic or weakly self-pitying. The last important contribution from the dream workers was to offer me suddenly, one night when I was milling over the poem in the dark, the image of blind Samson grinding the Philistine corn, an image which immediately linked itself with blind Milton in the miseries of his old age and the triumph of his enemies, writing *Samson Agonistes*. From this point on the poem was quickly finished and demanded no more than ordinary craft skill till it reached its final form.

As well as they can

As well as it can, the hooked fish while it dies,
Gasping for life, threshing in terror and pain,
Its torn mouth parched, grit in its delicate eyes,
    Thinks of its pool again.

As well as he can, the poet, blind, betrayed
Distracted by the groaning mill, among
The jostle of slaves, the clatter, the lash of trade,
    Taps the pure source of song.

As well as I can, my heart in this bleak air,
The empty days, the waste nights since you went,
Recalls your warmth, your smile, the grace and stir
    That were its element.

Poems are composed in many different ways but all ways involve a more or less complex interaction between what I have called the element of dream work and what I have called conscious craft work. I should have forgotten the details of this poem except that it stretched out over so long a period as to make the various stages of the process separate and evident. In poems composed more at a heat these stages often overlap one another and their outlines become blurred.

What distinguishes a poem of the sort I have just described from the dream-poems described before is that the latter lack the element of conscious control and deliberate shaping, without which they tend to remain incoherent and uneven, to the point sometimes of gross want of 'keeping'. On the other hand, poems that are wholly deliberate and conscious often turn out artificial and made to order, like the dreary and interminable Pindaric Odes of the seventeenth and eighteenth centuries. The element of creative play, of inventive imagination, is essentially a function of the dream workers, but, as we shall see in a later chapter, it is the element of serious and demanding craft work which stimulates and releases the dream work, as well as, in the long run, controlling it.

Critics and literary theorists, it seems to me, often go wrong because they start from the poem as a finished object and assume that it was planned and executed in this form and with this end in view. The anatomy of a poem, so to speak, is clear to them but its physiology, like its genesis, is hidden from them by the ultimate result of its processes that brought it into being. The material with which a poet works is precisely these processes.

4

Poetry and the Other Arts

The so-called Fine Arts obviously have many things in common. Perhaps the most fundamental of all is the fact that they represent the latest and therefore the still most precarious stage in biological evolution. Living creatures can be ranked in order of their living activities; at the bottom there is simply a vegetative sort of existence shared by plants and lowly animal forms alike. Higher animals add something: they are conscious and consciously directed, though usually under the direction of a specific pattern of instinctive behaviour; higher still, they show the adaptability that comes with self-conscious behaviour: the animal's environment is dealt with more by intelligent observation and variable learned behaviour than by set reaction patterns. Human beings have practically freed themselves from the latter and have achieved an intelligence and an emotional organization not only tied, as with most other animals, to the practical ends of survival and reproduction. Above all, they have invented a kind of activity practised purely for itself, the pleasure and illumination of mind and heart which we call art. It adds a new dimension to consciousness, it represents a new entelechy in the evolution of living beings. Man on the plane of art is in a freer world, and in a more comprehensive state of awareness than when he is pursuing the practical ends of living. Any of the arts can, of course, be made to promote these practical ends, but that is not their function or their nature. Their essential mode is joy, the contemplation and delight in what satisfies because it is beautiful. But while it partakes of the contemplative, art is something more, for it is essentially active, creative, participating, no matter whether we look at it from the point of

view of the artist or the audience. All the arts demand a
re-creative as well as a creative activity.

But if the arts share this common character, they are very
different among themselves. What sets them apart from one
another is in the first place the material in which the artist
works. The nature of this material sets a natural limit on
what the artist can do with it. Music cannot represent or
depict objects and events as painting can, nor can it express
ideas as poetry does; painting cannot convey narrative as
well as cinema or the novel can, and so on. Arts which
present themselves sequentially in time differ in radical ways
from those which present themselves with all their parts im-
mediately perceptible in space. Arts which present us with
an 'art object' differ in many important ways from those
which present us with, or require us to enter into, an 'art
activity', sculpture and dancing, for example.

Poetry in the European tradition has most often been
compared and classed with painting and music and a plaus-
ible argument can be set up for either view if it is based on
points of resemblance. But the moment one concentrates on
the points in which poetry differs from these arts, the case
ceases to be even plausible. Poetry, or rather literature in
general, is in a class quite by itself. Its dependence on a code
system sets it apart. Its peculiar position will become ap-
parent if we compare it with a selection of the main arts of
mankind.

It was perhaps natural that the two kinds of poetry which
Aristotle discussed in the fragment of a treatise on poetry
which has come down to us should have been described, in
visual terms, as imitations of men in action. Ancient Greek
epic and tragedy told a story and the subjects were mainly
chosen from myths or mythical history. Pausanias's *Descrip-
tion of Greece* written some six centuries later makes it clear
that Greek painting for many centuries in the past had had
the same subject matter. Aristotle's *Poetics* were lost during
the Middle Ages but the stage was set for Renaissance views
which tended on the whole to revive classical theories. Paint-
ing and sculpture imitate the world around, the visible
world, by means of paint or representation in stone or
bronze. Poetry does the same thing by means of words.
Horace's enigmatic 'ut pictura, poesis', added to the learned

confusion by suggestion that the principles on which poetry and painting were based, were, in fact, the same. Horace, of course, probably meant no more than that, if painters were allowed freedom to paint mythological scenes in different ways, then poets could be allowed to do the same. But the view that poetry was a sort of depiction by means of words stuck hard. Hamlet's description of the art of acting, 'to hold as 'twere the mirror up to Nature; to show Virtue her own Feature, Scorn her own image' and so on, is all in visual terms which are well enough for the stage, but easily come to apply to the play which the actors are presenting—a structure of words. Puttenham, one of the earliest of English theorists, speaks in his *Arte of English Poesie* of Homer's ability 'To paint out the speeches, countenance and manners of Princely persons'. The most splendid passage of Sir Philip Sidney's *Apologie for Poetrie*, where he praises the creations of the poets above those of Nature itself, represents poetry entirely in visual terms.

> Nature never set forth the earth in so rich tapestry, as divers Poets have done, neither with so pleasant rivers, fruitful trees, sweet smelling flowers, nor whatsoever els may make the too much loved earth more lovely.

Another instance of this unconscious bent towards equating painting and poetry is to be seen in the words we use to describe effects and methods in literature. The resort to pictorial terms in literary criticism is so usual that we are often unaware that we are using them metaphorically. We speak of the 'colour', 'brilliance' and 'texture' of one literary style, of 'obscurity' or 'flatness' of another, of the 'depth' of 'insight', the 'sparkle' of wit, the 'height' of inspiration, or the 'breadth' of imagination. I myself grew up with a feeling that poetry was primarily a method of making pictures with words and that imagery, particularly visual imagery, was what gave it life and force.

One has only to examine these traditional assumptions to see that they are false. A painting is extended in space; a poem in time. We take in a picture at a glance, even if we then study it in its details moving from one to another; we have to wait while a poem develops as music does. It is impossible to take it all in as a single momentary impression and this means that the relation of the parts to the whole are radically different in a painting and a poem. Much more important, however, is the fact that because the medium of poetry is a code system, it cannot have anything like the precise sensory impact of a painting, because language is conventional, that is, words are not *like* the things they denote, it can only give us an illusion, a sort of dream of what the painter can present directly in all its minute detail and exact colour. Moreover words, except for proper nouns, are always generalized, they stand for classes of things. If I say 'cat' the hearer may think of a very different cat from mine. Even if I go on to describe the animal with a wealth of detail, I will only narrow the range of ambiguity and abstraction. The painter can if he wishes show every detail, every hair, and present us directly with what language can never quite achieve, the individual, unique characters of the object, a particular cat. Language achieves its ends in other ways. No poet, not even Shakespeare, can describe the beauty of Juliet in such a way that any painter can present it directly, or that any two painters reading the poet's description could achieve more than a rough 'identikit' sort of likeness. Poetry achieves its ends by giving us the emotional equivalent, not the pictorial details:

> O she doth teach the torches to burn bright:
> It seems she hangs upon the cheek of night,
> As a rich jewel in an Ethiop's ear.

Even where the poet aims at precise visual detail he can only produce the impression of it, not the actuality. Set twenty painters to paint a tropical island from Tennyson's description in *Enoch Arden*, which has been rightly praised for its vivid evocation, and you will get twenty very different pictures:

> The mountain wooded to the peak, the lawns
> And winding glades high up like ways to Heaven
> The slender coco's drooping crown of plumes,
> The lightning flash of insect and of bird,
> The lustre of the long convolvuluses
> That coiled around the stately stems and ran
> Even to the limit of the land, the glows
> And glories of the broad belt of the world.
> . . .

The myriad shriek of wheeling ocean fowl
The league-long roller thundering on the reef,
The moving whisper of huge trees that branched
And blossomed in the zenith, or the sweep
Of some precipitous rivulet to the wave . . .

There is the illusion of precise and vivid detail here, but hardly more than that. Where is the observer standing in relation to the mountain and the beach? He is plainly standing (or sitting) under a huge tree but what species of tree and what is its foliage like? What kinds of insects and birds flash by and wheel about and what are their colours? What are the colours of the convolvulus? These are only a few of the questions any of our twenty painters would have to ask and to which the poem gives no answer. No, 'ut pictura, poesis' will not do in the sense in which the Renaissance took it. Somebody once called architecture 'frozen music'—not a very bright idea, but one with possibilities. No one, as far as I know, has yet ventured to call painting 'frozen poetry'. The visual and the verbal arts are totally distinct, both in the mediums they employ and in their modes of operation.

The principal rival of painting for an art so close that the two can be judged by much the same criteria, is, of course, music. The ancient Greeks used the same word for both, *Mousikē*, that is to say, an art combining both poetry and song (sometimes with an instrumental accompaniment). The association of the two arts was in part, at least, due to the fact that they had always gone together, a 'mixed art' like that of the theatre, where spectacle, poetry and dance and acting were combined. The assimilation of poetry to music has also continued to the present day and is especially associated with lyric poetry, for which the 'imitation' theory of Aristotle makes no provision—*The Poetics* breaks off before he gets round to this topic—but the assimilation is in many ways easier to make than in the case of poetry and the 'plastic arts'. Poetry, like music, is presented as a sequence in time. It has rhythm, and beat. It has sensuous auditory effects pleasing to the ear, so that we speak metaphorically of the 'music of verse'. It has modes and structures of metre and stanza which can be roughly compared with those of music, and in recent times there have been attempts to use verbal imagery to build up emotional structures without any explicit coherence as communication, on the analogy of the way music builds up structures of sound which are moving and satisfying in themselves without any content of ideas.

There is indeed an important sense in which a poem is much more than the communication of ideas; it *is* a structure to be enjoyed in and for itself on the analogy of music. But the comparison is no more than an analogy and is not in fact a very close one. I shall defer the consideration of the rhythmical, metrical and sensory aspects of poetry, merely pointing out that the sounds of poetry have nothing in common with those of actual music; they are not based on the sorts of relationship that exist between the notes of the musical scale. Moreover, as we shall see, the acoustic effects of which poetry is capable are impossible to unravel from the 'meanings' of the words. The notes and combinations of notes in music present us with pure tonal effects which have no symbolic meanings and no content of ideas. We can see this radical difference between the two arts if we imagine that the human race had decided to make the musical scale the medium of language, so that we literally sang our thoughts. Various musical combinations would then have had the function that words have now and what we call 'pure music' would then have been impossible, since it would have constantly suggested notions and ideas even though these had no coherent meaning. It would be like listening to surrealist verse with a musical background or texture.

We should remember, of course, that 'pure music' is a comparatively recent invention. The effects of music possible to complex instrumental or choral works are quite beyond the reach of poetry, which is only comparable, even if the analogy is admitted, to simple music for a single voice or single instruments. This follows from a fundamental difference between what is possible in music and what is possible in poetry. It is impossible to combine different verbal sequences in the way hundreds of instruments, melodic and harmonic lines can be combined in a great orchestra or even a string quartet. Try this with verse and the effect is one of confusion and mutual distraction. It is true that attempts have been made to combine different voices singing different words in choral works but what usually results is that the words are lost, or sacrificed to the music. We cannot listen to two lines of poetry at the same time, although we can listen to several melodic sequences at the same time and have no confusion between them; provided they are presented with the proper skill they only enrich one another.

During most of their history music and poetry seem to have supported each other, poetry supplying the 'meaning' or the narrative to the song, music enriching the verse, but in fact each remaining essentially a separate mode, not a mixed mode. My favourite image for the relationship involved in the setting of poems to music (because usually the text comes first) is to say that verse set to music is like the body clothed, adorned and enriched, but the clothes exist for the body and the body naked is more splendid than the body clothed. It was only at the end of the seventeenth century that music was freed from the dominance of the human voice and its limited range and began an independent career of its own. This development in the direction of 'pure music' has had the unfortunate effect of tempting poets and literary theorists in the last century and a half to develop various theories and sorts of pure poetry. The misunderstanding of the fundamental ways in which music and poetry differ will be matter for a later chapter. What Walter Pater meant by saying 'All art constantly aspires towards the condition of music' is uncertain, but the remark was influential enough to suggest a false analogy between pure music and pure poetry.

It is probably not worthwhile demonstrating the fact that another of the major arts, architecture, has very little in common with poetry and few have tried to do so. Critics sometimes use architectural metaphors, or speak of the architectonics of a large work like an epic, but the analogies are vague and do not seriously suggest that the two arts have anything in common. But architecture belongs to that group of 'applied' arts, in which the artist has to meet certain practical demands as well as produce a work of art in its own right. Such are the designing of the furnishing and utensils of a building as well as of the buildings themselves and their grounds and gardens, the arts of the dressmaker and tailor, the jeweller and even in some cases of the armourer and the cook. Improbable as it may seem, there have been attempts to associate poetry with some of these arts. Gautier's famous poem 'L'Art' became almost a manifesto for the Parnassian poets in revolt, in the second half of the last century, against the emotional excesses and careless workmanship of the French romantic poets. Gautier makes a serious plea for disciplined, detached and exact craftsmanship. But he makes no difference in kind between the craft of the poet and that of the jeweller, the sculptor, the worker in enamel, bronze, gold or silver.

> Oui, l'œuvre sort plus belle
> D'une forme au travail
> Rebelle
> Vers, marbre, onyx, émail*

As we have seen, there is a very important difference. The material in which jewellers and sculptors work is inert, inanimate matter on which the artist can work his will and exercise his skill. The material may be difficult to manipulate; it may not be easy for the artist to make it take the form he has imagined, but the material does not actually rebel. It is not alive. But the material of poetry is words, codified thoughts and feelings, part of the living processes of the poet's heart and mind. Poems take part in their own composition. Poets do not manipulate inert material; they co-operate in a living process.

At the beginning of our own century the Russian poets of the Acmeist group, in revolt against the vagueness and mysticism of the Russian Symbolists, proclaimed a doctrine of exact craftsmanship, clarity and precision of language and imagery. Gumilev, the leader of the group, translated Gautier's poem as a rallying point for the movement and made the same mistake as Gautier himself. It was the two greatest Acmeist poets, Anna Akhmatova and Osip Mandelshtam, who saw that language, the words of which poetry is made, cannot be treated as material like gold or ivory or marble. In a remarkable series of poems called *Secrets of the Craft*, to which I wish to return, Akhmatova reveals the real nature of the processes that go on in poetic composition.

Of all the more important arts of man it is perhaps dance, rather than painting or music, which has the closest affinity with poetry. The rhythmic structures of dance and poetry

* Yes, the work emerges more beautiful from a shape, verse, marble, onyx or enamel, which resists the craft.

are closer than that of either to music. Indeed both have traditionally used music to reinforce and enrich their simpler rhythms. Both painting and the other plastic arts, and even music, present us with what we may call an 'art object', a canvas, a statue, a musical work or a song. The process of making or producing the art object is quite distinct from the object itself. But with poetry and dance, the doing is itself the work of art. There is in a sense no art object, only an activity. With poetry there are two activities, the original thinking and feeling of the poet, and the encoding which is the means of transmitting and activating the complementary activity by which the reader or hearer re-creates and relives the experience—a sort of *pas-de-deux* for two or more persons. The poet is the partner of each of his auditors separately, whereas in many dances any number of people can join. As a poem uses the ordinary language we use for practical purposes but embodied in a rhythmical structure not used in ordinary conversation and communication, so dancing employs movements of the body, formalized and elaborated, set to rhythmical patterns unlike those we use in walking, running, bending or waving. And each is an activity whose end and satisfaction is in itself, not in an end external to it. To call poetry the dance of language brings out those aspects of it in which it differs from all other aspects and uses of language.

We think, perhaps, of the dance as an evanescent thing, whereas a poem has a certain permanence—Horace's

Exegi monumentum aere perennius*

has influenced us too much, as has the invention of writing. Before that dance, song and poetry were in the same boat— they are over with their performance and preserved only by being committed to memory and frequently repeated.

We tend to think of the dance, too, as something which cannot be translated into any other terms; it is strictly ineffable. I remember the remark attributed to Anna Pavlova when asked the meaning of one of her dances: 'If I had been able to put it into words, I would not have had to dance it.' Poetry, we think, ought to be translatable. Because it is in words it can be put into other words. But we only have to

---

* I have erected a memorial more enduring than brass.

try to do so to find that we have betrayed the original, or that
we have produced a real but another and inferior poem—this
is the insoluble problem of the translator of poetry.

In fact poetry is no more translatable than music or
dance. The experience that a poem is about, what it pre-
sents as its content, can be put into other words, but the
experience that the poem *is*, when we read or hear it, is in-
effable, for only the poem can be that experience. The dance
can be described, photographed, analysed; but only the
experience of having taken part in the dance is unique and
inviolable. It is the paradox of poetry, though self-evident
in the other arts, that every poem forms a unique experi-
ence *by means of words*, but one which can no more be put
into words than the experience of the dance or its accom-
panying music.

Literature, and especially poetry, is thus set apart from
each of the other arts in one respect or another; but there is
one thing above all that makes its position among them
unique. It is the fact that with all the others between the
artist and his audience there is the work of art, 'out there' in
the public world to be observed, discussed, assessed, enjoyed.
With poetry there is only the codified poem. With all other
arts there is the art object, a painting, a sculpture, a temple,
a jewel; or there is the art activity, a drama, a mime, a dance,
a song or an instrumental performance, to be observed or
participated in. The sensual impact of the other arts is
primary and dominant and direct. In poetry it tends to be
secondary and largely indirect. There is nothing 'out there'
except the codified poem ready to be translated back into a
mental experience, ready, I should say, to be re-created
as a mental experience similar to but not identical with the
poet's own mental process. The dance of language largely
goes on inside the head and it replaces sensory vividness
with a kind of controlled dreaming which in turn replaces
the hard, clear sensory impact characteristic of the other
art-objects and art-activities. Even the emotions of the inner
life, because they have to be transmitted in the same way,
are only spectres of the originals (the emotion of the poem
of which I shall have more to say later, is an exception). As
Wordsworth saw, and Byron wrote on one occasion to John

Murray: they are not the originals but a recall of emotion 'recollected in tranquillity'.

> As for poesy, mine is the dream of my sleeping Passions; when they are awake I cannot speak their language, only their Somnambulism, and just now they are not dormant.

Hume, who spent long periods of his life reflecting on what distinguishes 'ideas' from sensations, which he seems to have regarded as a more forceful and compelling sort of ideas, has summed the whole matter up very concisely in his *Enquiries Concerning Human Undertanding* (1777)

> All the colours of poetry, however splendid, can never paint natural objects in such a manner as to make the description be taken for a real landskip. The most lively thought is still inferior to the dullest sensation.

Poetry, of course, makes a direct sensory impact in one way and that is through its rhythms, its metrical and other beats. That will be the subject of the chapter which follows.

5

The Dance

Caliban: *Be not afeard, the isle is full of noises*
Sounds and sweet airs that give delight and hurt not:
Sometimes a thousand jangling instruments
Will hum about mine ears; and sometimes voices,
That if I then had waked after long sleep,
Will make me sleep again . . .

EVEN Caliban, in everything else so brutish, responds to
rhythm and music. The rhythms that enchanted him and
filled the island continually with sounds and sweet airs were
the result of magic, but we ourselves live from birth to death
surrounded and penetrated by an ocean of natural rhythms
which affect us and regulate our emotional life often without
our being aware of them. We can hear and feel our own
hearts beating; observers have recently discovered how
important for our whole emotional life is the nursing in
which a baby responds to the heart-beat of its mother; the
rhythm of our breathing reflects not only the energy we ex-
pend but also the emotional state in which we happen to be,
and our bodies observe hundreds of other rhythms, in-
cluding those of walking, running, skating and dancing. We
are aware of other pulses in the world around us: the sound
of the sea, the changes of day and night, of the seasons, the
tides, the rising and setting of sun and moon and stars, the
beating of drums, the rhythm of machinery, the sound of a
train, a plane or a car, the voice of a choir or an orchestra.
We are continually immersed in so many rhythms that
poetry takes a natural place in the symphony of the world.
Nothing is less artificial than metre. Its rhythms are based
on those of life itself.

All rhythm is based on some kind of alternation and hu-
man speech has a number of these, all of which form part

of the total rhythmical effect of poetry. The simplest of these is the alternation of sound and silence in the flow of speech; then, in most languages, there is an alternation between the more strongly stressed and the more lightly stressed syllables; there is another alternation in most languages between syllables that are long and others that are short. In nearly all languages there are variations in pitch or intonation, with a consequent alternation of high, medium and low tones, with as many as eight or ten distinctions of tone in some. These are distinctions we all recognize because at one time or another one or more of these alternations has been made the basis of a metrical system. What is still not recognized is that the sounds of which words are composed differ in quality and timbre and that in consequence these form a natural alternation with a rhythmic pattern of its own. Some languages develop an awareness of separate consonantal and vowel patterns—English is such a language and most poets are conscious of 'vowel harmony'   within a line and of a separate pattern of consonants, resulting in conscious effects such as alliteration or onomatopoeia. From eastern Europe to the Pacific a large number of unrelated languages feel a contrast between what are called 'soft' vowels and consonants and 'hard' ones which makes for a subtle interplay and alternation in the texture of speech. A Semitic language such as Arabic makes an even more subtle distinction between consonants into 'sun letters' and 'moon letters' and further complicates the patterning of sounds.

In ordinary speech, in prose, these patterns are more or less random and the rhythms are irregular; we are not concerned with them directly, we are concerned with the meaning of what we say rather than the sound effects. But in verse, probably because this is the only way poetry has of making a direct sensual impact, these elements of rhythm become extremely important. We are made aware of them in the first instance by a deliberately chosen pattern of repetition which we call metre. It has been customary to talk about the rhythms of ordinary speech as natural and to imply that metrical rhythms are by contrast artificial. I do not believe this; we breathe in metre, our heart beats in metre, we walk, run, skip and swim in metre and there is nothing artificial about these activities. If we speak in metre, we merely adapt language to another but quite natural pattern.

Any of these alternations could be chosen as the basis of the repeated pattern we call metre. In the European tradition two have predominated: counting by stresses and counting by length of syllable or quantity. Latin is a language which seems originally to have had a very archaic system of counting by stresses, the two-stave alliterating measure which was also preserved by the Germanic languages and of which there are faint traces in very ancient Greek and in Sanskrit. Under the influence of Greek and the prestige of Greek civilization, Roman poets adopted *quantity*, the alternation of long and short syllables as the basis of metre but later partly abandoned it during the Middle Ages in favour of stress metres. By then Latin was a dead language, but its enormous prestige as the language of religion, learning and literature had a great influence on the metrical systems of the colloquial languages of Europe including English. English poetry at first was written in the old Germanic two-stave alliterative metre, the metre of *Beowulf*, and in various later developments of it such as we see in poems like the Old English *Judith*, the Middle English *Piers Plowman* and *Sir Gawayne and the Grene Knight*. Some time in the fifteenth century this ancient traditional type of metre died out, or was assimilated to new metrical schemes based on Latin, French and Italian measures. The latter underlie the system most familiar to us and still in use today. It consists of various patterns formed by the alternation of stressed and unstressed syllables. When the same foot is repeated a certain number of times, we have a 'metre'. One of the simplest of such feet, an unstressed syllable followed by a stressed syllable, is the foot called an iambus. Repeated five times this gives us the familiar English metre, iambic pentameter:

> If all the pens that ever poets held
> Had fed the feeling of their masters' thoughts,
> And every sweetness that inspir'd their hearts,
> Their minds and muses on admirèd themes;
> If all the heavenly quintessence they still
> From their immortal flowers of poesy,
> Wherein, as in a mirror we perceive
> The highest reaches of a human wit;
> If these had made one poem's period,

And all combin'd in beauty's worthiness,
Yet should there hover in their restless heads
One thought, one grace, one wonder at the least,
Which into words no virtue can digest.

A great many misconceptions about metre exist and more tend to arise. One consists in thinking, as I used to when I was young, that the rhythmic structure of poetry is metre, and that what Dryden calls 'the other harmony of prose' has another irregular and quite different rhythmic arrangement. As a consequence of this belief, and of theories of scansion based on Latin and Greek verse, a conviction arose that the pattern of repeated 'feet' of the same kind should be kept as strictly as possible. Any deviation was a licence, necessary perhaps to avoid the deadly monotony that ensues if verse is strictly metrical, but still a derogation of the ideal. It is a point of view that recalls the philosopher's joke: 'This is the best of all possible worlds and everything in it is a necessary evil.'

Of course the whole idea is absurd, but it took me long years to see it. Metre is like the time signature in music. It is an abstract pattern, giving the hearer an expectation of a constant return to the beat and a constant reassertion of the pattern, but in English verse this pattern is constantly varied and these variations may be carried quite a long way, short of breaking down the principal pattern altogether. Even Marlowe, whose lines from *Tamburlaine* I have just quoted, though he observes the iambic pattern quite closely, after four quite 'regular' marching lines, puts a little trip into the march with the extra light syllable in 'heavenly' and a softer footfall on the last syllable of 'quintessence', which is only nominally a stressed syllable. Three lines further on, by giving a nominal stress to the quite unstressed 'of', he introduces a similar tripping effect on the steady march with three light syllables together. He repeats this flutter in the steady beat with

hover in their restless heads

and then, with the effect of a couple of great waves at the climax of this long verse paragraph, he introduces three extra stresses in

One thought, one grace, one wonder at the least

before falling back into the expected metrical pattern. Not
only is there elasticity and variety in this verse but in the cli-
max line which should break the metre, the expectation of
the five-beat line is not disappointed; we hear it through and
syncopated against the actual scansion. It is this delicate bal-
ancing of metre against scansion which is one source of the
rich effects of rhythm possible in English verse.

At the other end of the scale the variations on the expected
pattern become so continuous and pervasive that the pattern
is all but swamped in the variations. Consider this example
taken from W. H. Auden's *The Shield of Achilles*.

> After shaking paws with his dog
> (Whose bark would tell the world that he is always kind),
> The hangman sets off briskly over the heath;
> He does not know yet who will be provided
> To do the high works of justice with:
> Gently closing the door of his wife's bedroom,
> (Today she has one of her headaches)
> With a sigh the judge descends his marble stair;
> He does not know by what sentence
> He will apply on earth the Law that rules the stars:
> And the poet, taking a breather
> Round his garden before starting his eclogue
> Does not know whose truth he will tell.

Auden is one of the most dexterous and inventive tech-
nicians of our day. Here all that remains of the iambic penta-
meter is that there are mainly five stresses in each line. The
extreme variation of the placing of unstressed syllables has
almost obscured the pattern, which only briefly shows itself
here and there: 'whose bark would tell the world. . . . He
does not know yet who will be provided . . . the judge de-
scends his marble stair . . . He does not know by what . . . the
Law that rules the stars. . . .' The sense of a marching line has
almost but not quite been lost. This perhaps is as far as
verse can go without dissolving into prose.

Between these extremes poets have a generous and in-
deed almost an endless variety of choice. It is a complete
mistake to imagine that metre is restrictive, or results in the
monotonous repetition of a single simple pattern. And
several other devices extend the range of rhythmical possi-
bilities till they are literally unlimited. One of these is the

imaginary or actual pause in a line which we call caesura (cutting). Although Marlowe's verse tends to have a steady marching beat and a majority of lines are end-stopped, which increases the effect, it is by no means monotonous. In addition to the metrical variations we have noted, the caesura is constantly moving its place. In the first eight lines of the speech quoted above the pause occurs after the fourth, the fifth, the sixth, the second, the ninth, the sixth, the second and the sixth (since a line may have several caesural pauses) and the fifth syllable of the ten or eleven syllable line.

The lines of verse themselves form units of larger rhythms, those of the verse paragraph and the stanza. Lines may be end-stopped or 'rove over' so that sense runs straight on into the next line. This gives a further wide range of variety in the rhythms. The use of lines of varying length within a stanza gives a wider range still, as does the great variety of possible rhyme schemes in rhyming verse.

I should turn aside here for a comment on rhyme, which has commonly been misunderstood as a device in poetry. In the first place, ever since the Revival of Learning, the prestige of Latin and Greek poetry, which did not use rhyme, tended to make scholars and scholar poets despise it.

Everyone remembers Milton's magisterial condemnation in his preface to *Paradise Lost:*

> The measure is English Heroic Verse, without Rime, as that of Homer in Greek, and of Virgil in Latin; Rime being no necessary adjunct or true Ornament of Poem or good Verse, in longer Works especially, but the Invention of a barbarous Age, to set off wretched matter and lame Meeter; grac't indeed since by the use of some famous modern Poets, carried away by Custom, but much to thir own vexation, hindrance and constraint, to express many things otherwise, and for the most part worse then else they would have exprest them.

This view of rhyme as a mere tawdry and useless ornament, what Milton goes on to call 'the jingling sound of like endings', did not, fortunately, prevail. English poets continued to use rhyme and showed no sense of 'vexation, hindrance and constraint', right down to our own day, when the devotees of free verse have mostly abandoned it, with the other craftsman-like skills.

E

Rhyme, we may agree, is not a necessary device. Poetry can get along without it. But the fact that so many unrelated languages all over the world have independently adopted it, suggests that it is more than a trifling ornament. It is, in fact, a part of the rhythmical structure, a device of regular return to a fixed point similar to the device of metre itself. The alternation of sounds of differing quality or timbre, the vowel and consonant alternations, form an irregular rhythm, though not a random one, for a good poet always pays close attention to their arrangement. At regular intervals, usually at the end of the line, rhyme introduces a regular rhythm into this aspect of the pattern. When the line is end-stopped it gives an extra emphasis; where the sense and syntax run on into the next line it marks the end of the rhythmic sequence or unit that constitutes the individual line. One cannot help thinking that Milton was disingenuous when he said that poets who use rhyme are forced 'to express many things otherwise and for the most part worse' than they would otherwise have expressed them. He himself used rhyme with superb ease and felicity and he must have had experience of the fact that in the search for rhymes that must fit in perfectly and naturally, the poet often hits on things *better* than he would have expressed them at the first-heat.

If Milton chose to ignore this, one of his predecessors, stout old Samuel Daniel, knew it and had cleared his mind of neo-classical cant: in his *Defence of Rhyme* he comments on the fact that English is rather poor in rhymes, as an advantage:

> And indeed I have wished there were not that multiplicitie of rymes as used by many in Sonets, which yet we see in some happily to succeed, and hath been so farre from hindering their inventions, as hath begot conceit beyond expectation and comparable to the best inventions of the world: for sure in an eminent spirit whome Nature hath fitted for that mysterie, Ryme is no impediment to his conceit, but rather gives him wings to mount, not out of his course, but as it were beyond his power to a farre happier flight.

I like to think of the poet using rhymes as fish-hooks in this way, and I should like to think myself one of Sam's 'eminent spirits' fitted by Nature for that craft and mystic knowledge,

for Daniel is using the word 'mystery' in both the senses it
then had. But whether I qualify or not I am convinced that
rhyme and its adjunct alliteration are very important ingre-
dients in the Dance of Language. Alliteration has, like
rhyme, been treated as a trifling ornament instead of being,
when used discreetly and aptly, one of the most powerful
adjuncts of the rhythmical structure of verse.

But we have so far considered only the variety and the
range of the elements that comprise the regular or metrical
rhythms in all their richness and we have not even touched
on that other beautiful and complex habit of English verse
by which the ear counts by the number of stresses in the line
but constantly varies the number and arrangement of the un-
stressed syllables. This is the principle on which so many of
the nursery rhymes are based, so that we 'tune in' to both
principles in early childhood. The regular one is represented
by a rhyme like

> Sing a song of sixpence,
> A pocket full of rye;
> Four and twenty black-birds,
> Baked in a pie.
>
> When the pie was opened,
> The birds began to sing;
> Was not that a dainty dish
> To set before the King?

This is regular verse metre, trochaic and iambic in alternate
lines.

But another old favourite, 'Tom, Tom the piper's son',
though its last three lines are in regular metre, has its first
two built on another principle which English has always
known, the principle of counting by main stresses and allow-
ing a variety of arrangements of the unstressed syllables. This
was the principle on which old alliterative stave verse was
constructed. It is the principle of some of Shakespeare's most
delightful songs.

> Where the bee sucks, there suck I
> In a cowslip's bell I lie,
> There I couch when owls do cry,
> On the bat's back I do fly
> After summer merrily:

> Merrily, merrily, shall I live now
> Under the blossom that hangs on the bough.

It is a kind of verse that Coleridge imagined himself to
have invented for *Christabel*, 'founded on a new principle:
namely, that of counting in each line the accents, not the
syllables'. It is a principle of which Gerard Manly Hopkins
gave an account which suggests that he, too, thought he had
discovered it. He talks of 'sprung rhythm' as opposed to
regular metre, which he calls 'running rhythm'. On the
whole, in English verse this type of rhythm has usually been
subordinate to regular metre and there are great possibilities
still to be explored in it.

But so far we have paid only slight attention to what
most contributes to the inexhaustible resources of English
verse, and that is the fact that when we read or recite poetry
we read it 'according to the sense', that is to say according to
the divisions and units of rhythm that are characteristic of
prose. In good verse these are arranged so that they do not
contradict or obstruct the metrical rhythm but, in Hopkins'
phrase, are 'counterpointed' against it, or as he says,

> ... the super-inducing or *mounting* of a new rhythm upon the
> old; and since the new or mounted rhythm is actually heard
> and at the same time the mind naturally supplies the natural
> or standard foregoing rhythm, for we do not forget what the
> rhythm is that by rights we should be hearing, two rhythms
> are in some manner running at once and we have something
> answerable to counterpoint in music, which is two or more
> strains of tune going on together, and this is Counterpoint
> Rhythm.

Hopkins in this passage of his preface to a manuscript of his
poems, is actually talking about the accepted metrical vari-
ations in regular verse, but what he says is even truer of the
counterpointing of the prose rhythms against those of the
verse, which I have called the actual scansion, to distinguish
it from the abstract pattern which I have called the metre.

Prose is composed of rhythmic units, corresponding to the
'feet' of verse, which follow the sense and natural punctua-
tion. Prose feet never cut words in the middle as verse feet
often do. Thus a line like

> Devouring time blunt thou the lion's paws

has as its metre iambic pentameter. This of course is simply the ideal pattern. We never read it as

Devou - ring time - blunt thou - the li - on's paws

which would sound ridiculous. Nor do we even keep to the actual verse scansion, though the poet has made sure that we hear this verse rhythm syncopated against the prose rhythm which is what we actually say:

Devouring - time - blunt thou - the lion's - paws

By these few and quite simple means the endless complexity of the dance of language is made possible. But we have explored only the mechanics of the system and only the general principles at that. Children at school and students at universities often find the mechanics of verse a barren subject. It is, they find, more complex and subtle than they had been led to expect. But this does not explain why it attracts; the mere schemata of verse hold nothing to give a clue to the magic and fascination that they are able to evoke. For that we must consider the marriage of rhythm and meaning which makes the evocation possible.

Before I do so, however, I should like to say something about the claims of so-called free verse to replace metrical verse with a superior product.

6

The Dance and the Shuffle

THIS should be a short chapter, as I have given my views
on the claims of free verse elsewhere.* I called the article in
question *Free Verse: A Post-Mortem,* at a time when I
thought I detected encouraging signs that this tedious and
essentially trivial movement was on the wane after fifty years
of claiming to be the young, progressive, up-to-date and
fashionable approach to poetry. I was, as it turned out, quite
mistaken. Free verse today is not only the major and most
common form of poetry but it has captured most of the
magazines, the editors, the publishers and at least two-thirds
of the academic pundits in those fifty years. The child who
told the emperor he had no clothes on grew up to be the
professor who lectured on the exquisite embroidery of *The
Waste Land* and the *Cantos* of Ezra Pound, thus giving a
respectable pedigree to this bastard child of prose, practised
by most of my younger contemporaries today.

However it is easy enough to make fun of this effete and
spurious heir of the great House of Poetry. All I wish to do
is to point out once again the grounds of its inferiority and
the hollowness of its claims to inherit and displace the true
lineage.

When anyone uses the dangerously ambiguous word 'free',
my immediate impulse is to ask: 'free from what?' The
libertarian ideas of the nineteenth and twentieth centuries
have accustomed us to thinking of any sort of freedom as a
positive good, any kind of liberation a step forward. This is
simply not so. We can be as easily freed from the demands of
conscience or commonsense as from those of tyranny or
false shame. Sometimes freedom means the gain of some-

* *The Cave and the Spring,* Adelaide, 1965, pp. 38-50.

58

thing precious or essential to human life or dignity, at other times it can mean the loss of the same treasures. This is so with free verse. It is not verse, because it contains no principle of repetition, or regular pattern. It is true that free verse cuts up slabs of prose into artificial lines where the habits of readers, based on genuine verse, suggest a break or pause. But unless these pauses occurred at points where syntax naturally suggest pauses they have no rhythmic meaning, and if they follow the pauses of syntax they are simply a new way of writing prose. In fact, nine-tenths of free verse can be arranged in any way one likes without making any difference. To test this it is only necessary to print it as prose and ask readers who have not seen the poem before to put it back into its original line arrangement. The result is about what you would get by throwing dice. The alleged verse of 'free verse' is an optical illusion, a mock up of poetic shape on the page, without the essential form of verse to give it substance. When read or recited aloud this illusion largely disappears, for the ear cannot distinguish where the so-called lines of verse begin and end, as they can when guided by the scansion and rhymes of genuine verse.

The claim of those who favour free verse is, of course, that by getting rid of regular metre and scansion it has been able to create a new series of rhythms, which form sequences giving expression to the individual nuances of the thought in individual poems, whereas, they affirm, the old generalized metres could not do this; in them the thought had to be fitted to an already existing and stereotyped pattern, instead of finding its own appropriate rhythmic form. As the manifesto of the Imagist Movement half a century ago put it, their aim was

> To create new rhythms—as the expression of new moods—and not to copy old rhythms which merely echo old moods. We do not insist upon 'free verse' as the only method of writing poetry. We fight for it as a principle of liberty. We believe that the individuality of the poet may often be better expressed in free verse than in conventional forms.

It would be hard to find more fallacies and errors packed into so brief a statement. As we have seen, free verse creates nothing new: it is limited to the rhythms of prose, and its artificial line arrangements only exist on paper and have no physical basis at all. There is no way of reconstituting them from a version printed as prose. Moreover these 'new rhythms' already form part of the old rhythms. Prose rhythm is an essential ingredient of regular verse and the source of at least half its variety and richness of effect. All the free verse poet has done is to deprive himself of half the resources that poetry puts at his disposal. The idea that the purpose of poetry is to 'express moods' is an inheritance from the Romantic thesis that poetry was a form of self-expression, a revelation of the poet's emotions. This will be dealt with in a later chapter. The fight for free verse as a principle of liberty seems unexceptionable: poets should be free to try any method they like. But there is an implication that those who practise regular verse do so in chains. This is simply a confession of ignorance of the real nature of regular verse which, in turn, is the result of confusing it with metrical pattern. Once we have seen, as in the last chapter, the almost unlimited variety and scope for new invention that traditional verse allows, it seems a puzzle to know what the freedom of free verse consists in. I once described the limited rhythmic effects of free verse as those of people trying to dance without music, and limited only to the steps used in walking. It would be, I said, a dreary shuffle and for the most part that is just what it is. What it 'frees' the poet from is grace, elasticity, the sense of dance and the sense of song. One might as well talk about freeing a bird from the tyranny of its wings. Forced to walk, like Baudelaire's albatross,

> Ces rois de l'azur, maladroits et honteux,
> Laissent piteusement leurs grandes ailes blanches
> Comme des avirons trainer à côté d'eux.*

There is an element of verse in 'free verse', as there is usually an element of walking and running in the dance, but, cut off as it is from the free flight, this liberation from pedestrian ends, we could more properly describe 'free verse' as 'deprived verse' or 'hamstrung verse'.

It is natural to ask, of course, why free verse has proved so popular. Several things I believe have contributed to this. In the first place it is obviously popular with poets. There is

---

* These kings of the azure sky, clumsy and embarrassed, let their great white wings drop miserably beside them like oars.

little evidence from the sales of books of poetry that it is popular with readers. The number of books published is no guide in this country, where most volumes of verse are subsidized directly or indirectly from public funds. I believe that in the first place it is popular with poets, especially young poets, simply because it is *easy*. It takes years of hard work to master the techniques and learn to explore the possibilities of metrical verse; anyone who is not 'word-deaf' can learn to turn out free verse that will pass muster with its devotees in a few weeks. I know because I have practised both sorts in my time. I gave up free verse in the first instance because it bored me; in the second because with no fixed point of departure and return, its unlimited variety of rhythms resulted in monotony. And lastly I gave it up because I was tired of being confined to a shuffle when I preferred the enjoyment of the dance. As for the alleged freedom that this sort of verse was said to confer, I was certainly free to say what I liked in any way I liked, but there seemed no means of deciding between one way and several others. I was free to choose but had no criterion of choice. I came more and more to see that real freedom lay within a discipline and that mastery, which is the only freedom worth anything to an artist, cannot be achieved without discipline or, as Goethe put it so magisterially in '*Natur und Kunst*':

> Vergebens werden ungebundne Geister
> Nach der Vollendung reiner Höhe streben.
> Wer Grosses will muss sich zusammenraffen;
> In der Beschränkung zeigt sich erst der Meister,
> Und der Gesetz nur kann uns Freiheit geben.*

But at the age I then was, I knew nothing of Goethe. I had to grope my way slowly and doubtfully against the popular current of the day, guided more by feeling than any clear answers to the arguments of the Imagists and torn by my admiration of Hilda Doolittle, who did manage to make free verse work at times by using parallel prose rhythms and repeated effects of cadence, as does the prose of the *Book of Common Prayer*.

No doubt more young poets would prefer the hard discip-

---

* Spirits unconstrained will aspire in vain to the pure heights of perfection. He who wishes to do great things must draw himself in; only in self-concentration is mastery revealed and Law alone is able to give us freedom.

line but for another siren voice that beguiles them. They naturally like to think themselves in the swim. Free verse has not only been advertised as liberating the poet but also as promoting him. It is the modish and *avant-garde* medium. The young poet feels that he is taking part in the great forward movement in all arts, unaware that whatever progress painting or music may have made in the past half-century, the result of the very limited possibilities of free verse was that it exhausted its possibilities very early and has been marking time ever since. Dance can build on dance, one opening new possibilities for another, but you cannot develop much of a shuffle except another shuffle almost indistinguishable from the first.

But perhaps the most compelling force at work is the loss of sensibility involved. The poet who works at the hard but rewarding task of marrying the metrical and the prose rhythms is continually educating his ear, building up habits of distinguishing the best from the better, or the merely passable. The poet who is content with the mediocre effects of free verse not only never develops and refines his sensibility', he actually deteriorates and loses the power to distinguish the higher qualities of traditional poetry. His ears habituated to prefer the shuffle soon lose the power to appreciate the dance.

I could go on, but there seems no point in doing so. It is a pity to see the waste of talent involved but it is comforting to reflect that bad poetry cannot last. It carries within itself its own principle of built-in obsolescence as surely as the motor cars and refrigerators and television sets which manufacturers of today design and build so carefully not to last too long. To adapt Pope's triumphant lines on Timon's villa:

> Another age shall see the golden Ear
> Imbrown the slope and nod on the Parterre,
> Deep Harvests hide their rotting contraband,
> And laughing Ceres re-assume the land!

7

Sound and Sense

To set down the full rhythmic structure of any line of poetry we would have to produce something like a musical score for several instruments. In the left-hand corner of the page would be some device to indicate the particular basic metre, corresponding to the 'time signature' on a musical score. The first line would consist of a notation of the scheme of this regular metre, divided into the necessary number of feet. Under this the actual scansion of the line, indicating the reversed and substituted feet and those introducing extra hyper-metrical syllables, or leaving one blank. Under this again the various prose rhythms, the groupings of words by sense and syntax, including indication of the caesural pauses, the alternations of length of syllable (or quantity) and, in addition another line to indicate the pitch rhythms. These three though they are different qualitative effects, follow the pattern of the prose feet. For indicating pitch we would need something equivalent to the signs for increase or decrease in volume, to indicate the effect we call cadence and the special rhythmical effects of light, swift movement or slow and ponderous movement, which are partly an effect of syntax and partly of the length of words. The contrast of long and short words creates a special rhythmic effect of its own.

Lastly, we would need two lines to indicate the sequence of vowel and of consonant harmony and contrast with a notation to indicate special effects such as alliteration and rhyme.

All in all, it would be a formidable piece of orchestral scoring. Its use might be to demonstrate to critics who do not take all this into account, just how complex the rhythm of verse is and just how much variety and freedom poets have within the so-called bonds of metre. But it could have the less useful effect of suggesting that this analysis of the rhythmic elements is what a poet has to work out separately or what his audience has to attend to separately and assemble for themselves, as we are conscious of and attend to the various instruments in an orchestra. The fact is that these are all elements in a single rhythmic impression which we attend to as a whole. As for the poet, he has to learn to be conscious of the effect as a whole but he is rarely aware of the details of his 'score', he works by habit and trial and error, until he recognizes the effect he is searching for; then everything slips into place and any further change is for the worse. Form and content have become an inextricable and unanalyzable whole. It is this sense of the magical and inevitable 'rightness' of good poetry which authenticates it for its composer and his audience. It is a sense that a poet can only learn by patience, persistence and alertness. There are no rules for it and no prescriptions; because one has to be able to recognize the 'rightness' of something not existing before the moment of its emergence, and often in a context not yet clear to the composer. The composition of a poem is a series of epiphanies.

It is partly for this reason that it is so hard to say anything illuminating or even sensible about the way sound and sense are related in poetry. Nothing is purely sensory and nothing is purely notional. Beauties that we are inclined to attribute to the effects of rhythm, even in what seems a case of obvious onomatopoeia, may get most of their feeling, in fact, from the meaning of what is being said. I used to try to illustrate this to my students by taking Tennyson's lines:

> The moan of doves in immemorial elms
> And murmurings of innumerable bees.

which, with its setting of a drowsy summer afternoon, has been rightly praised as an example of verbal music and metrical felicity. But if you change three sounds in the second line

> And murdering of innumerable fleas.

all the delicious effect of sound echoing sense seems to vanish. It is the sense that lends the sound most of its effect.

Metre, and the complex of rhythms it organizes, undoubtedly work on us independently of meaning; the pulse and throb, the bound and rebound of the recurrent stresses work on us as other forms of percussion do; and it must have done so much more in the past, when poetry was usually spoken or sung aloud to the accompaniment of music and dance. Its action can be described as hypnotic; it isolates and elevates the mind; it puts it into a special attitude towards the subjects of poetry which can be compared to the special attitudes to religious practice induced by the ceremony, the liturgy, the singing, the vestments, the archaic language of the service and Bible, the ecclesiastical architecture, stained glass and incense in the minds of the worshippers. Its second effect is that of release and inducement to 'let oneself go', to participate and to enter into a higher state of awareness, as some forms of religious dance are used to provoke ecstasy and even mystic experience. On the side of the composition of poetry I have already mentioned its function in helping the crystallization of a poem once it gets under way. Not only does the preoccupation with fitting prose sense to metrical rhythm so that both seem perfectly natural, help to elicit new images and better forms of words and to allow the poet to achieve what Ben Jonson called striking 'a second heat on the Muse's anvil', but it also acts, I have found, as an organizer of the still amorphous structure of the poem and a touchstone in choosing and rejecting what comes into the mind as offerings from the dream workers. Why this should be so I cannot say; I only note it as a constant factor in composition: the moment one stanza has taken shape the whole mode of composition changes. One works consciously to repeat the pattern laid down.

One must not insist too much, of course, on the sensory effects of rhythm in poetry. It is a mild intoxicant compared with the heady effects of music or the vigour and excitement of the dance. Coleridge justly observed of it in the eighteenth chapter of *Biographia Literaria:*

As far as metre acts in and for itself, it tends to increase the vivacity and susceptibility both of the general feeling and of the attention. This effect is produced by the continual excitement of surprise, and by the quick reciprocations of curiosity still gratified and still re-excited, which are too slight indeed to be at any one moment objects of distinct consciousness, yet become considerable in their aggregate influence. As a medicinal atmosphere, or as wine during animated conversation, they act powerfully, themselves unnoticed.

For the most part, however, it is my experience that metre does not simply 'act in and for itself': its main function is to interact with the meaning of what the poem is saying and in turn to have the meaning react on our sense of metrical effect. What we think we hear, as in the 'murmuring of innumerable bees', is a sort of dream transference from the situation suggested by the words to the rhythms themselves. In fact, while the rhythms have a sensory impact and an emotional evocative force of their own, most of their effective force comes from association. We can observe the rhythms of poetry in a language we do not know and react to them in themselves but when we do this as I remember doing in listening to an expert re-evocation of the pronunciation of Homer, or to a modern Urdu poet reading his verse, we know that we are missing the flesh to which this rhythmic structure is no more than a skeleton.

Apart from its actual sensory impact the rhythm of verse shares the code-system of language, and is indeed an integral part of it. 'The sound must seem an echo to the sense'; This dictum of Pope's, one of the most delicate and skilful observers of metre among English poets, may be accepted if we put the emphasis on the word 'seem'. This is evident from the examples he gives:

> When Ajax strives some rocks vast weight to throw
> The line too labours and the words move slow:
> Not so when swift Camilla scours the plain,
> Flies o'er th' unbending corn and skims along the main.

The effect claimed for these operations of rhythm is certainly there, but how much of it is due to the sound itself and how much to the sense producing its illusion of an echo? We recall that a little earlier in the same passage of the *Essay on Criticism* Pope had used a line made up of monosyllables of about equal stress:

> And ten low words oft creep in one dull line:

to give the effect, not of ponderous and immense effort, but of flatness and creeping dullness. One recollects, again, that a little earlier the effect of an iambic hexameter used among pentameters gave the effect of sluggish and dreary movement:

> A needless Alexandrine ends the song,
> That, like a wounded snake drags its slow length along.

Whereas now, with Camilla, Pope makes it suggest swift, light and airy motion. Analysis of the rhythmical structure of the two lines, both in metrical scansion and in prose groupings, shows that they are almost identical except for the inverted foot followed by a spondee in the first instance, after the caesura. The caesura itself falls in the same place. The effects of slow and swift movement in the rhythm come almost entirely from suggestion derived from the sense of the words in each case and not from the rhythms themselves. I am tempted to wonder if the most famous of all examples of the sound echoing the sense, Virgil's

> Quadrupedante putrem sonitu quatit ungula campum*

would produce the same onomatopoeic effect, if in the previous line, not a troop of galloping horses had been in question but the slow plod of Tuscan draft oxen to which the line could equally apply. It might even fit better, since *we* tend to read the line as though it were in stress metre; the less forceful effect of the quantitative metre might favour the tread of the oxen.

In any case, and in passing, it is worth remarking that these examples are an illustration, if any was needed, of the absurdity of the claims of the addicts of 'free verse', that metre confines the movement of thought within stereotyped effects, or that a pattern appropriate to that of the individual thought and feeling is impossible within its predetermined rhythm.

In fairness to such claims, however, I must admit that so far I have discussed the rhythms of traditional English verse mainly in terms of iambic-trochaic metres. With the tripping, cantering and galloping metres, those we call anapestic-dactylic, the metrical beat is much more dominant and the prose groupings more likely to conform closely to the metrical pattern, instead of contrasting with it and being syncopated against it. The first two lines of Byron's 'The Destruction of Sennacherib' have as their metrical scansion:

* Hooves with their four-footed beat shake the crumbling plain.

> The Assy - rian came down - like the wolf - on the fold,
> And his co - horts were gleam - ing in pur - ple and gold;

while the prose rhythm grouping is:

> The Assyrian - came down - like the wolf - on the fold,
> And his cohorts - were gleaming - in purple - and gold;

It is harder to hear the prose rhythm against the stronger beat of the metre and, in fact, the latter almost demands that we reduce the strong stress that in normal speech we would put on 'came' and 'like' in the first line and on the second syllable of 'cohorts' in the second.

On the other hand, in poems where mixed metre has more or less taken over, so that one counts by stresses rather than by 'feet', the prose rhythms tend to predominate, as in R. L. Stevenson's:

> In the highlands - in the country - places,
> Where the old, plain men - have rosy - faces,
> And the young Fair - maidens -
> Quiet eyes;
> Where essential - silence - cheers and - blesses,
> And for ever - in the hill - recesses
> Her more lovely - music -
> Broods - and dies.

We are far away here from any obvious or crude effects of matching sound to sense and yet this beautiful stepping and pausing rhythm seems an essential part of the meaning. What each contributes to the total effect and what each contributes to the other, it is, I believe, impossible to analyze. Because it is impossible to analyze, and because of the infinite variety of ways in which sense can influence sound and *vice versa,* no rules can be built on the analysis, we can formulate no recipes or technical generalizations, as is possible in music. Every effect in poetry is individual and unique and poets have to learn their craft by testing each line by ear, trying one variation after another till it sounds just right.

The ability to master this wholly pragmatic skill depends not only on constant and patient practice but also on the poet's constantly reading, soaking up and repeating the poetry of the past (from which he learns the basic tradition) , and the poetry of his contemporaries, from which he learns to 'make it new', as Ezra Pound says. If he is any good,

however, he will treat the contemporaries with caution, if
not with suspicion, for the fashionable voices may absorb and
drown his own. He will write, as T. S. Eliot said, 'not
merely with his own generation in his bones, but with a
feeling that the whole of the literature of Europe from
Homer and within it the whole of the literature of his own
country has a simultaneous existence and composes a simul-
taneous order.' This is perhaps demanding too much, and
certainly more than is necessary. Eliot was, perhaps, too
much influenced by the practice of the late Symbolists in
France, of which Eliot's own poetry shows a damaging
influence, and of whom A. M. Schmidt says:

> Ils fouillent toutes les littératures, depouillent à la hâte tous les
> rituels, dressent des répertoires de pseudo-symboles, afin de les
> utiliser au besoin.*

A poet does not have to be erudite in this way and the eru-
dition of poets is different from that of scholars. A good
poet does not need to have the *whole* tradition in his bones,
nor to have it in any systematic way. He feeds here and there
as his nature draws him. But without a sense of the tradition,
at least in part, he will never acquire the instinctive skills to
make those choices which renew and find new resources in
poetry. Eliot's main contention is perfectly sound.

One reason for this is that the rhythms of verse have, in
the course of centuries, acquired effects and significances
which are not inherent in them but have grown to seem
so by association. This is a character they have in addition to
the associations they acquire in individual poems, to which
I have just been referring. These are associations which
properly belong to the metres, the stanza forms and the
modes of poetry themselves. By custom and consent such
associations, both in poetry and music, seem to have been
formalized in ancient Greece; so that certain forms and
metres, like certain musical 'modes', were automatically as-
sociated with certain subjects, certain emotional responses
and certain literary forms, such as drama, epic and lyric.
Aristotle takes it for granted that each genre has its metre:

> With respect to metre, the heroic is established by experience
> as the most proper, so that, should anyone compose a narrative

---

* They ransack all literatures, strip all rituals bare and amass a repertory
of pseudo-symbols, in order to make use of them as required.

F

poem in any other, or in a variety of metres, he would be
thought guilty of great impropriety . . . But the iambic and
trochaic have more motion; the latter being adapted to dance,
and the other to action and business. To mix these different
metres, as Chaeremon has done, would be still more absurd.
So no-one has ever tried to compose a lengthy [narrative] poem
in any other than heroic verse; nature, itself, as we remarked
before, having indicated the proper choice.

Nature, of course, having left the hexameter behind,
could not care less, but English poetry is in any case not
quite like this. Yet in thinking of the problems of sound and
sense there are some vague assumptions that should be
taken into account or the whole picture may be distorted.
English poetry has never developed a feeling that a par-
ticular metre is appropriate only to a particular type of
subject or a particular literary mode. The Earl of Surrey,
looking for a suitable medium for his translation of parts
of the *Aeneid,* chose unrhymed iambic pentameter verse. It
had little success, except in the theatre, and none as a
medium for epic poetry until Milton chose it for *Paradise
Lost.* In spite of the fact that Milton calls it 'English heroic
verse without rime', thereby equating it with the classical
hexameter, it was never exclusively associated with epic
poetry, and Milton's implication that in the seventeenth
century it was generally recognized as the proper metre for
epic was of course a piece of genial bluff. No-one but Surrey
had used it for that purpose and Surrey's translations of
Books two and four of the *Aeneid* had long fallen into ne-
glect or oblivion. Its stiff versification had been replaced by
the usage of dramatists like Marlowe, Shakespeare and Jon-
son. It seemed an adaptable and handy metre for purposes as
different as Milton's description of the war in Heaven,
Wordsworth's account of his student days in Cambridge or
Shakespeare's use of it for stage dialogue. No other metre,
and no stanza form as far as I know, has ever come to be
associated with one type of composition or subject-matter.

Nevertheless all practising poets know that the negative as-
pect of this is true. Certain metres do seem inherently un-
suitable for, or incompatible with, certain sorts of subject,
mode or mood. An elegy in the metre of 'How We brought
the Good News from Ghent to Aix' would be incongru-

ous. A funeral should not go at a brisk gallop or even a
canter. Iambic-trochaic pentameter is rarely used for lyric
or 'singing' verse, and where it is, as in Tennyson's 'Tears,
Idle Tears, I know not what they mean', its success has some-
thing of the effect of a *tour-de-force*. Conversely, light and
tripping metres seem inherently unsuitable for poems of
sustained reflection, description or narrative. Despite Gold-
ing's *Ovid* and Chapman's *Homer*, the fourteeners so popu-
lar in sixteenth century English verse, and especially their
use in the infamous Poulter's Measure, seem now not suit-
able for anything but comic verse and burlesque. Surrey's
love poems in this measure remain only as curiosities of
literature.

Most poets tend to have favourite metres and stanza forms
though few, perhaps, could say why they have particular
preferences. But one of the most mysterious things in the
composition of poems is the question of why one chooses
to write in couplets, in stanzas or, in blank verse, when setting
out on a particular subject or theme. Poe's ridiculous account
of how he came to write 'The Raven', by deduction from
first principles does not touch on this. He seems to have
chosen the metre and stanza form not with regard to the
subject but simply in order to display his virtuosity. This is
a pity because, in spite of an inhumanly mechanical method
of composition, Poe's discussion of the process of crystalliza-
tion of a poem has some interesting insights. All that emerges
from his account is that at the moment when he had the
ingredients of his poem and its mood generally in mind, at
the point where he began to bring these general ideas to-
gether and to give them specific form in words, he also de-
cided on a specific metre and stanza. The interesting thing,
perhaps, is that the poet does not attempt to tell us why his
particular choice of forms seems to him the most appro-
priate. In every other particular of the composition he is
pedantically anxious to explain why his treatment is the
best. It would appear that the choice seemed to him so ob-
vious that it needed no explanation. From my own observa-
tion, this would appear to be so. There are occasions when
I have chosen to write in a set form like an sonnet or *ottava
rima* because the unwritten and vaguely conceived poem
appeared to me in this form. On most occasions, however, the

form emerges with the subject, as though the emergent poem chose and developed its metre and stanza at the same moment that the emerging poetic structure began to define and select the detail of the treatment, the images, the general flow and direction of thought and feeling. At other times a single line or image will come into my mind unforeseen and apparently by chance and this will have its own rhythmical shape on which the rest of the poem continues to grow. I have described on another occasion how the poem 'Imperial Adam' grew in this way from the first line, which, when the dream-workers idly pushed it up into consciousness, seemed like so many verse lines recalled from actual dreams, to be nonsense.*

More often than not subjects seem to choose their forms and all I can say is that one develops a sort of instinct for helping the process, without as a rule knowing just how or why the combination occurs.

Because the inter-relations of sound and sense in poetry are so hard to pin down, or to describe convincingly, I have occasionally tried to account for them in terms of an analogy, and I shall end this chapter with one of them, to which I return from time to time. One can either think of it as an elaborate metaphor or as a simplified mechanical model designed to free the main features from the mass of much more complex but confusing detail. That is, after all, one of the functions of a metaphor. If the analogy seems crude, that, too, is part of its purpose, so that no-one will be tempted to take it too literally.

All my life I have enjoyed and delighted in travelling by train, particularly at night, when I can lie half-awake for hours borne along on its rhythms in spirit as literally as I am carried along bodily. The sounds of a running train in the days of steam were dominated by two main regular rhythms. The first of them was the clickety-click, clickety-clack of the wheels on the bogies at each end of the car passing over the small gaps at the junctions of the rails. This was a complex rhythm, because against the loud clacking of the nearest set of wheels one could hear the same sound repeated in diminishing loudness from the wheels farther ahead and behind and when the train was going at speed

* *The Cave and the Spring*, pp. 78-80.

the Doppler effect gave a different pitch to the sounds coming from behind and ahead, and the rhythm was of course constantly varying with the speed of the whole train. It was by no means a monotonous and unvaried beat; but it was *regular*, in that it contained an unvarying principle of expectation which was never disappointed, even when the wheels ran over a set of points which introduced a new and louder rattling beat. There was, and still is, to me something of the enchantment of metre in it and I used to try to fit words to it. With the train tackling a long upgrade the rhythm was the clearly defined clickety-clack! and I would find such idiot rhymes as:

> Clickety clack
> Over the track
> O my delight
> Now we run right
> On through the night
> Into the black
> On through the night
> Turn off the light
> Kiss me good night
> Cuddle me tight . . . etc.

Nonsense of this sort seemed, in fact, to be generated by the wheels themselves.

When the train was on a downgrade, or going very fast across level ground, the rhythm would seem to reverse itself and the pause between one clickety-clack and the next being hardly perceptible it turned into the well-known metre of the old knee-rhyme:

> To market, to market to buy a fat pig,
> Home again, home again, jiggety jig
> To market, to market, to buy a fat hog,
> Home again, home again, jiggety jog.

The second main rhythm was that of the puffing engine, always pervasive but hardly noticed most of the time in the general roar and rattle of the hurrying train. When pulling out of a station, and especially when labouring up through mountains, it became especially clear, a four beat rhythm with the stress on the first beat, or so it seemed: *chuff*, chuff, chuff chuff—*chuff*, chuff, chuff, chuff. As the engine turned from side to side along the winding track, this rhythm was continually rising and falling in intensity and changing in pitch and tone as the train entered cuttings or emerged onto open embankments. The two main rhythms were not actually connected at all, but the effect was of one syncopated against the other and producing in my mind an effect of rich and soothing and at the same time exciting and anticipatory harmony, to which were added all the *irregular* rhythms of the moving train: the different echo-effects from tunnels, bridges, cuttings of perpendicular stone and glacis slopes of gravel, clay, or earth, the amorphous but constantly varying roar of our progress through the night and the countless small clinks, groans, clatters and shocks of the car itself, the bumps of the couplings and the constantly changing pitch of the flanged wheels against the rails as they took the strain of the curves or spun along the level stretches. I used to lie hour after hour analyzing these sounds and identifying them, but in general they formed a single tonal and rhythmic impression, just as in the *tutti* of a great symphony we can distinguish the various instruments and their contribution to the whole, and yet apprehend the music as a total effect.

Complex and richly varied as the train symphony is, it is also, of course, a purely mechanical series of sounds, without purpose or meaning in itself. In this it differs from the performance of a symphony orcheestra, even though the orchestra, like the train is proceeding along rails, the rails represented by the musical score. The interesting thing is that for the boy in the sleeping car the train rhythms did have meaning and purpose; the idea of the journey, the element of exploring and adventure. The boy's mind contributed this to the mechanical rhythms and the mechanical rhythms supplied a physical basis to the dream of travel. It all took place unconsciously, in the sense that it did not have to be planned or contrived, nevertheless it was a perfectly conscious, experience, indeed at times a state of ecstatic awareness.

The last point of my analogy is this sense of being only one element in a process over parts of which I had no control, of fusions and combinations going on in which I was participating more than directing. I was being 'borne along' with the train. Many a time in composing a poem I have had this sense of participating, of being carried along with its growth rather than choosing the direction and holding the driving wheel. A critic who has not had this experience will always be limited when he comments on the finished poem. I find most of the books that talk about prosody and the technical details of verse arid and unsatisfactory for this reason.

In the composition of short poems, of course, one may be more aware of the problems of getting under way. By the time the fundamental rhythmic structure has been established, its journey of a few stanzas may be too short for the processes I have just described to emerge clearly. It is in the composition of a really long poem, one that must be taken up and continued for days or even years, that one becomes most aware of being on the train. The rhythm and metre then become almost independent of the poet and in addition a sustaining and generating force and source of ideas and images.

8

The Language of Poetry

WHEN we talk to one another, we do not usually have much trouble in finding the words and the forms of expression we need, even though we may on occasions find ourselves at a loss for a word. The expressions we need come to our lips automatically and in a continuous flow, as though they were being supplied from a store-house and adapted to the need of the moment by some vast computer system. The computer we call the brain has a great store of linguistic expressions capable of being adapted on the spot to any particular occasion but essentially 'ready-made'. Nine-tenths of what we say in ordinary conversation consists of formulas. We are like skilful tennis players adapting a limited number of strokes to a continually varying number of situations of defence and attack.

When a poet composes the one-sided conversation we call a poem, he is doing something similar. He is drawing on a great store of formulas, as any user of language must do, but the process is much less automatic, very much less stimulated and directed by the unknown other partner, who has not yet, in fact, entered the conversation, and though the poet may not be at a loss for a word or a phrase, he often has to pause as though he were, because he is aware that every word in his poem exerts a force on every other word and modifies its meaning or its power to evoke feeling. This is something that does not as a rule worry us in the ordinary business of communication. This 'interinanimation of words', as Coleridge called it, is the poet's main technical pre-occupation. As his practice and his skill increase, he is able to hand over a good part of it to his habits, to his sub-conscious supervision and selection. If he does he may, at the best, fall into what Gerard Manly Hopkins, writing of Wordsworth, called a 'Parnassian style', 'that is the language and style of poetry mastered and at command but employed without any fresh inspiration', or he may end by parodying himself like Swinburne or, at worst, drift into the mindless sludge of surrealist verse.

Because a good poem is an integral whole and some of the inter-connections it establishes are so subtle as to be undemonstrable, the complete texture of inter-inanimation is difficult to describe, but its main features can quite easily be shown by a paraphrase. In a paraphrase the main ideas, feelings and sentiments remain, but the overtones are apt to be lost, the intimate links between one word or image and another are either broken or replaced by others not so effective, and the metre and rhythm, even if they are preserved, lose the effect of miraculous rightness and aptness that marks the marriage of sense and sound that I referred to in the last chapter. 'Beauty', said Blake resides in minute particulars, 'and it is by comparing the minute particulars of the paraphrase with those of the original that the inferiority of the paraphrase can be used to illuminate the beauty of the original in all its details.

We can imagine Coleridge who was a very unequal poet, composing during the night a stanza which he added to the original version of "The Ancient Mariner" ' a stanza describing the sudden and dramatic onset of night in the tropics:

> The Sun's rim dips; the stars rush out:
> At one stride comes the dark.

Although Coleridge had never witnessed this, the lines have been rightly praised for the truth and beauty of the description. Now let us imagine that next morning, when not at his best, Coleridge endeavours to recollect the stanza, which he had neglected to write down the night before, and comes up with this:

> The Sun's edge touches; stars leap forth:
> In one jump night arrives.

This preserves the general idea; but is without magic; it is flat verbiage and lamentable verse. What has happened? The most obvious failure is with the personification of night. In the original it is a swift and terrible continuous march of the dark, here a more appropriate word than 'night', because it has behind it echoes of the sinister aspects of night, a hint of powers of darkness which is reinforced by the evil let loose in the poem as a whole. In the second version not only is night a neutral word but the 'jump', as opposed to the 'stride', introduces a comic suggestion irrelevant to the general effect intended. The word 'touches' loses the sense of downward motion of the sun over and below the horizon and 'stars leap forth' is a feebler image than the rush of stars from the suddenly darkened sky: the sense of sudden *release* is replaced by a mere gymnastic display. The light disyllable of 'touches' replacing the stressed monosyllable of 'dips' weakens the effect of the repetition of rhythm in the two halves of the line and displaces the caesura, so that the onomatopeia of great striding steps suggested by

> The Sun's rim dips
> The stars rush out,
> At one stride comes . . .

is almost lost and with it most of the interplay of rhythm and meaning.

This illustrates the way the overtones of words work. But the close integration of meanings and rhythms can be illustrated in another way. The result of using less effective words is one thing: the result of using less effective rhythms is another. On the whole the metre is preserved in the second version and the result is poetry of a sort, a poor and enfeebled version but preserving some quality of poetry. See now what happens if we, in fact, turn the lines into free verse:

> The rim of the Sun dips,
> Out rush the stars,
> The dark
> Comes at one stride.

It is clear that without metre the inter-inanimation of the words is greatly reduced. Once again the general meaning is the same but the special effect, or quality, we call poetry has evaporated. At best it is only a poor, pale, etiolated residual effect. This should be a last nail in the coffin of free verse, since it demonstrates one important function of metre in making words combine so that their overtones link and reverberate. It is this combination that has the effect or quality we call poetry.

What, in fact, we have been witnessing is something in the nature of a small control experiment with the various elements of which poetry is composed, varying one ingredient in each case while keeping the others unchanged. The analogy is not exact, because each of the elements interacts with the others in such a way that to change one is to change them all. Nevertheless we can learn from such demonstrations the sort of contribution that each of the elements makes to the whole.

I have often thought that the part played by metre and the nature of what we have been calling the 'inter-inanimation of words' could be illustrated by analogies from chemistry. A mixture of the two gases hydrogen and oxygen is one in which the qualities of each remains what they were before, but pass an electric spark through the mixture and part of it will form a chemical substance, H_2O or water, which has qualities not possessed by either gas or by the mixture of the two. All the characters of ice and snow, of clouds and mists, rainbow and shower, of lakes and rivers and seas are implicit in the electro-chemical bond that links two atoms of hydrogen with one of oxygen. Metre is like the electric spark: by organizing the energies of the various rhythms of language it enables emotional bonds to form between the overtones and fringe associations of words and images, over and above their dictionary meanings and the syntactic bonds of grammar. A new quality not possessed by its individual elements characterizes these combinations and it is to this quality that we give the name poetry. In part metre provides the 'energy' necessary to enable the bonds to form, in part it acts like a catalyst of the sort which speeds up and intensifies reactions which would not go on, or would go only slowly and weakly, without them. Metre has an equally important function in inhibiting and excluding irrelevant associations, in encouraging fruitful ambiguities and discouraging disruptive or side-tracking ones.

In the case of the half-stanza on which I have made this little experiment I could strengthen the analogy because John Livingstone Lowes has been able to detect, from Coleridge's reading, the various separate elements which com-

bined to produce the poetic effect, a sentence from Mary
Wollstonecraft's *Letters Written during a Short Residence
in Sweden, Norway, and Denmark* about the stars 'darting
forward out the clear expanse' as the moon rose; another
phrase from a travel book about the West Indies at the time
of sunset: 'the sun is no sooner dipped than . . .'; yet an-
other from Bruce's *Travels*: 'As soon as the sun falls below
the horizon, night comes on and all the stars appear'; and so
on.* Here, as in the case of oxygen and hydrogen, the ele-
ments neither together nor singly have the extra and pecu-
liar quality they have in the combination. We ought not to
forget that the analogy is no more than that: something of
the sort does seem to happen in poetry, but words and
rhythms are not substances. Their combinations are in-
finitely varied and cannot be reduced to formulae like those
of chemistry. A poet works by habit and instinct and the
qualities he achieves are each time unique, new and unpre-
dictable. Chemists sometimes have the same delightful
experience but on the whole their hypotheses are based on
known regularities and their results are quite predictable.
Those of poetry are more often effects of shock or surprise.

Translators of poetry have to wrestle not only with these
unpredictable effects of inter-inanimation but also with the
fact that no two languages are alike in the overtones and
suggestions which words even of the same dictionary mean-
ing, have in each. But poets and translators are usually more
acutely aware of these overtones than readers. I have some-
times tried to make my students more aware of them by
writing what is more or less a translation of a good English
poem into other English. I would choose an original not
likely to be familiar to them and put the two versions side
by side without comment and would ask them to compare
the two. Once I took the first stanza of Thomas Campion's
exquisite poem, the twentieth in his *Booke of Ayres:*

> When thou must home to shades of underground,
> And there arrived, a new admired guest,
> The beauteous spirits do ingirt thee round,
> White Iope, blithe Helen, and the rest,
> To hear the stories of thy finished love
> From that smooth tongue whose music hell can move.

* *The Road to Xanadu,* pp. 162-3.

Alongside this I set my 'translation':

> When you arrive in the dim underground,
> And there at last, a fresh and welcome guest,
> The ghosts of lovely women gather round,
> Fair Iope, glad Helen and the rest,
> The whole tale of your loves to hear you tell
> In that soft voice whose notes please even in hell.

The inferiority of the second version is immediately apparent to any sensitive reader, but the exact reason for this may not be so and the subtler reasons may escape notice or be impossible to state in detail. But some failures of inter-inanimation are easy to detect. The word 'home' in the first version has so many more overtones that link it with other parts of the poem, than the word 'arrive' in the second. 'Home' is in itself a more richly suggestive and evocative word. In this context it evokes the return of the soul to its natural place of origin after the journey of life, reinforced by such older phrases as 'man goeth to his long home' 'Thou thy earthly task hast done, home hast gone and ta'en thy wages' or later instances such as Shelley's 'those poor slaves . . . who travel to their home among the dead' or Stevenson's 'home is the sailor, home from the sea'—for one of the fruitful gifts of a literary tradition is that poems grow in evocative power from all that follows as well as all that precedes them in time. Not only are there these general associations and suggestions for the word 'home' to draw on, but in this particular poem the beauty whom the poet is addressing finds herself immediately 'at home' in the company of her peers, the great beauties of the world who lived before her. 'When thou must home' has overtones of the inevitability of death and its finality which are quite lacking in the phrase 'when you arrive'. 'The dim underground 'stresses only the darkness of the next world: 'shades of underground' catches this and links up, because of its other meaning, with the 'spirits' of the next line; 'spirits', again, has suggestions of liveliness, of spirited action which links with the picture of the beauties of the past gathering round for some delighted feminine gossip. Ghosts never gossip and the word would not be as effective as 'spirits' in this context. 'Fair Iope' cannot compete with 'White Iope'; the chime of the vowels in the sec-

ond case has an ineffable felicity the first cannot match and
the white limbs animate and are animated by the shades
of the first line, not only with a superior visual image but
also with a sense of invincible beauty in the house of death
which links up with the invincible joy of 'blithe Helen'.
'Blithe' is altogether a stronger word than 'glad' here, partly
because it suggests a permanent disposition, whereas glad-
ness may be no more than a temporary state of mind. 'The
stories of thy finished loves' is more expressive than 'the
whole tale of your loves', because the latter lacks the explicit
overtone of the end to all the delight of the world which
death entails and, because of other implications of the word
'finished', it suggests something of exquisite or polished
workmanship. This leads on to a link with the 'smooth
tongue whose music hell can move'. The smooth tongue not
only suggests a beautiful voice and charming speech, but
has overtones of flattery and deceit which link up with and
emphasize the poet's anguished cry in the last line of the
poem:

Then tell, O tell, how thou didst murder me

Moreover it connects with the rich ambiguity of 'whose
music hell can move'. The inversion leaves us uncertain
whether we are to take it as, 'whose music can move the
underworld and its powers,' as that of Orpheus did, or as
'whose music can be inspired or animated by hell'. In fact
it is to be taken in both ways and the christian word 'hell',
replacing the gentler notion of the classic underground, is
a prelude to the theme of agony and evil in which the poem
is to reach its climax. None of this is suggested by the cor-
responding line of the alternative version.

Such is the way the inter-inanimation of words functions.
Coleridge's famous distinction of the language of fancy and
the language of imagination admits of argument and to
many, such as myself, seems to be a matter merely of degree
rather than of real difference of kind. But what Coleridge
called the *esemplastic power* of verbal synthesis under the
bonding influence of metre—for he too used an analogy from
chemistry—was one of the greatest advances in critical in-
sight since the beginning of critical theory itself.

The inter-inanimation of words is, of course, not confined

to poetry. It is characteristic of every use of language, except those lifeless and repulsive jargons which some writers, particularly social scientists, feel obliged to invent for themselves. This is why it is impossible to deny free verse some share in it. But where it adds grace to ordinary uses of language, it is not the main object of communication as a rule; in poetry on the other hand, organized and transfigured by metre it undergoes a sort of apotheosis and becomes that essential quality of language which we distinguish by the name of poetry. It becomes a second voice above that of communication of ideas and feelings. It is, of course, an integral part of that communication, but in what it adds to the whole it has the character of what it has lately become fashionable to call a 'meta-language'—a bastard formation on the model of 'metaphysics', itself an erroneous derivation, but nevertheless a useful word for a notion not previously supplied with one. As a meta-language it is the chief conveyor and producer of the emotion *of* the poem as distinguished from the emotion or emotions *in* the poem. This is a subject to which I must return in a later chapter. It will be enough here to illustrate the difference, which can easily be done when the two emotions are in sharp contrast. When Catullus in his rage addresses the drinkers in the *salax taberna* where his faithless mistress is sharing her favours with all, or when Donne pictures himself appearing as a ghost to terrify *his* faithless mistress in bed with her lover.

When by thy scorn, O murdress, I am dead,

the emotions in both poems are anger, jealousy, contempt, frustrated desire and bitter self-pity, but the emotion of the poem itself in each case is a sort of delighted irony, the artist's enjoyment in his own creation, the contemplative pleasure afforded by a perfect work of art (and perhaps the satisfaction of a perfect revenge).

Another meta-language, not by any means confined to poetry but more at home there than in any other use of language, so that it seems native to it, is that of the devices which have in common the comparison of one thing with another: metaphor and simile, personification and its shadow apostrophe, analogy, allegory, symbolism and their opposite numbers, parody, puns and homophones, caricature, antithesis and oxymoron.

Here we are on fairy-ground. Nine-tenths of the words in daily use have a *doppelgänger*, a ghostly partner or partners yoked to the meaning actually intended by the fact that the 'same word' is used for both. Whenever a word extends its meaning, which words are constantly doing, the spectre of a comparison is set up. Wherever homophones occur there is already waiting the suggestion of puns or other plays on words and not always for comic effect. Lady Macbeth's remark as she goes back to Duncan's murdered body with the bloody daggers:

> I'll gild the faces of the grooms withal,
> For it must seem their guilt

is not only a shocking play on words that adds greatly to the horror of the scene but there is also a further sinister implication in the association of 'gold' and 'guilt'. When Othello holding the light above the sleeping Desdemona says:

> Yet I'll not shed her blood,
> Nor scar that whiter skin of hers than snow,
> And smooth as monumental alabaster . . .

the overtones of snow and alabaster add to the visual impression the reminder of Desdemona's chastity and the image to be carved on the tomb she is so soon to occupy. When Horatio says to Marcellus after the account of the ghost of Hamlet's father:

> But look, the morn in russet mantle clad
> Walks o'er the dew of yon high eastern hill,

the personification adds to the picture of the red light of dawn the reminder that Aurora is a goddess, here pictured as a country girl wearing a coarse reddish brown cloak as she makes her way over the dewy hillside. It is a wonderfully evocative image of freshness, peace and simplicity, coming as it does after a feverish and disturbed night.

It is a mistake to think of such devices, including metaphor and simile, as 'ornaments' of poetry, though this is a common way of treating them. They are integral to the way poetry works. It becomes a second language allowing a concentration of meaning and a richness of texture that none of the other arts can reach to. None of the other arts, indeed,

has the metaphysical resources of poetry, by which one thing
is constantly used to illuminate another and is itself illu-
minated by the comparison. Comparison, seen aright, is of
the very stuff and texture of the poet's art: a means of say-
ing what cannot be said by any form of direct statement. It is
a way of extending the limits of experience and feeling
beyond what they are capable of by any other means.

But in the profoundest poetry these metaphysical resources
go further. They not only make the things compared illu-
minate one another and fill the mind and heart with a sense
of those mysterious correspondences in nature which en-
chanted the young Baudelaire, they also give us insight into
something beyond either of the things compared or con-
trasted. 'I question not my corporeal or vegetative eye' said
Blake, 'any more than I would question a window concern-
ing sight. I look through it and not with it.' It is this power
to make a poem a window which we look *through* and not
merely *at*, which distinguishes the higher power of poetry;
it is on this that the intellectual force of poetry depends, and
it is through the mastery of this that poetry lays claim to be
a unique and higher mode of comprehension, a special mode
of vision. It opens the way to feel bondings and relations
and harmonies, which do not depend on outward resem-
blances at all. As Hölderlin's Hyperion exclaims:

> Ihr Quellen der Erd! ihr Blumen! und ihr Walder und ihr
> Adler und du brüderliches Licht! wie alt und neu ist unsere
> Liebe! Frei sind wir, gleichen uns nicht ängstig von aussen;
> wie sollte nicht wechseln die weise des Lebens? Wir lieben den
> Äther doch all und Innigst im innersten gleichen dir uns.*

This ecstatic passage would have given Blake no trouble at
all and Baudelaire might have accepted it. But its romantic
mystique apart, it expresses perfectly the central function of
comparison in the language of poetry.

Comparison is, of course, not a device essential to poetry,
though it does lend it wings. One of the most perfect short
lyrics in the language does without it:

---

* You springs of the earth! you flowers! and you forests and you eagles and
you fraternal light, how old and new is our love! We are free, we do not
resemble each other in narrow outward qualities: how should the mode
of life not vary? Yet we all adore the aetherial fire and in the innermost
selves within we resemble each other. (*Hyperion*, Book II).

G

> Western wind, when wilt thou blow,
> The small rain down can rain?
> Christ, if my love were in my arms
> And I in my bed again.

But no poem of any length can avoid it.

This is an immense, an endless subject and its use and control is the constant study of poets and sometimes their despair. A great part of the metaphors inherent in language are what we call dead metaphors. A mathematician speaking of the 'square root' of a number, a housewife 'rooting' through the junk in her attic, a doctor explaining to his patient the root of trouble he is having with his digestion, are none of them likely to think of the root of a plant or to need to do so in order to make their meaning perfectly clear. But because poetry works more with overtones of words, the dead metaphors constantly tend to come alive, the inter-inanimation of words brings the comparison back to notice, sometimes with disturbing, or comic or disruptive effect. When Macbeth asks his doctor,

> Can'st thou not minister to a mind diseased,
> Pluck from the memory a rooted sorrow?

the cliché 'rooted sorrow' becomes a live metaphor by the influence of the word pluck which restores the image of the plant. Cowley was not so happy in his description of Lot's wife as she was changed to a pillar of salt:

> She tried her heavy foot from ground to rear,
> And raised the heel, but the toe's rooted there.

The metaphor is reanimated with incongruous effect. Even Shakespeare, in careless moments, can do the same thing, as he does in the speech from which I have just quoted:

> Cleanse the stuffed bosom of that perilous stuff
> Which weighs upon the heart.

Where the two senses of the word 'stuff', both of them metaphorical react on each other to produce an effect worthy of *The Stuffed Owl* itself.

In considering the language of poetry, we should say something about diction. We have already noticed that English poetry knows nothing of the special dictions appropriate to particular literary forms or types of subject which were Aristotle's concern in Greek poetry. For all that, every practising poet is aware that the tone of a particular poem depends, at the very least, on avoiding words which appear out of keeping, with the rest. Dr Johnson's view that a 'high' style is necessary for tragedy is probably correct in a general way. When we are in the mood of

> Once again the fierce dispute
> Betwixt damnation and impassioned clay
> Must I burn through;

that mood is likely to be disrupted by consciously comic, facetious or colloquial language. On occasions when the latter would be appropriate, the language of tragedy might appear pompous or out of place. But we appear to have lost the sense of 'keeping' that prompted Johnson's protest at Shakespeare's 'low' language in the passage in *Macbeth*:

> Come thick Night,
> And pall thee in the dunnest smoke of Hell,
> That my keen knife see not the wound it makes,
> Nor Heaven peep through the blanket of the dark
> To cry, hold, hold.

To Johnson's sensibilities the use of 'knife' and 'blanket' in such a context was comically inept. We probably have Wordsworth's campaign against 'poetic diction' to thank for our surprise and Wordsworth's protest was probably justified by a great deal of the inane and mechanical mannerisms of late eighteenth century poets. Pope's exquisite,

> With hairy sprindges we the birds betray,
> Slight lines of hair surprise the finney prey,
> Fair tresses Man's imperial race insnare
> And Beauty draws us with a single hair.

is itself betrayed when inferior scribblers will never descend to talk of fish except as 'finny prey' or of goldfish as red-gold; it has to be

> Their scaly armour's Tyrian hue
> Thro' richest purple to the view
> Betrayed a golden gleam.

(Gray, of course, is playing with, or making fun of, the convention). But Wordsworth's insistence on the ordinary language of men, 'a selection of language really used by men', to say nothing of his preference for a modified form of the language used in humble and rustic life, has tended to impoverish the resources of poetry and, after nearly two centuries, has left the poets of today too timid to venture much outside the limits of contemporary colloquial speech. A poetic diction, used mechanically, is certainly vicious, but used intelligently and sensitively it can produce poetry of the highest order. Two of the greatest poems in the world, *The Iliad* and *The Odyssey*, the foundation of our whole European literary tradition, are written, so the scholars tell us, in an artificial literary dialect which nobody ever spoke and for the most part in stock phrases which the poet pulled out of a capacious memory and adapted to his purpose. Two great English poems *The Faerie Queene* and *Paradise Lost* are written in an artificial literary diction invented by their authors. Poets as diverse as Chatterton and Gerard Manly Hopkins have done as much for their admittedly minor but successful performances. The feeling so ingrained in the minds of many poets today that they must limit themselves to colloquial speech and avoid 'literary' vocabulary and syntax is no more than a superstition and cuts them off from the riches accumulated by the tradition. Language cannot live unless it breathes, and the air it lives in is common speech. It must constantly return to this or poetry becomes a dead language. But neither is it bound to common speech. Its time-span embraces the whole space in which the language is viable—in our case from Chaucer to the present day—and a poet who is free of this vast territory is not bound to limit himself to one of the frontiers. Ever since I became aware of the debate, I have confronted Coleridge to Wordsworth.

Wordsworth: 'It may be safely affirmed, that there neither is, nor can be, an *essential* difference between the language of prose and metrical composition.'

Coleridge: 'Metre in itself is simply a stimulant of the attention, and therefore excites the question: Why is the attention to be thus stimulated? Now the question cannot be answered by the pleasure of the metre itself; for this we have shown to be conditional and dependent on the appropriateness of the thoughts and expressions to which the metrical form is super-added. Neither can I conceive any other answer than can be rationally given, short of this: I write in metre because I am about to use a language different from that of prose.'

I have not cited this debate at random. The modern theory of poetry begins with Coleridge, as the modern practice of poetry begins with Wordsworth. When the two clash, I come down on the side of Coleridge. He weakens his case by using an idea he borrowed from Wordsworth, that after the poet had conceived his poem and planned it he began work by turning this, presumably, prose version into metrical form. Metre was then 'superadded'. It was Coleridge's fatal mistake to adopt this absurdity. For all we know about Wordsworth inclines us to believe that he never *superadded* metre. The poem and the metrical form grew together, and, as we have seen, one prompts, guides and regulates the other. It is an indissoluble process working both ways at once. But because of this error, Coleridge has not quite given Wordsworth the answer that Wordsworth already knew. 'I write in metre, because I am about to use a language different from that of prose.' That answer can be given by an analogy: that diamond is *not* simply carbon with a crystal lattice 'super-added'. The crystal arrangement of the carbon atoms in the diamond lattice gives the gem qualities which the amorphous forms of carbon do not possess: qualities of extreme hardness, brilliance and transparency. In somewhat the same way language organized and animated by the regularities of metre acquires qualities which prose does not possess. The vocabulary and the syntax may be the same but it is already a language different from that of prose, without any resort to a special poetic diction. And once this is admitted, Wordsworth's contention that 'there neither is or can be any essential difference between the language of prose and metrical composition', loses its force. The tradition of poetry, moreover, gives a wider choice than is open to prose in the matter of language. As Coleridge went on to argue:

> The true question must be . . . whether in the language of a serious poem there may not be an arrangement both of words and sentences and a use and selection of (what are called) figures of speech, both as to their kind, their frequency and their occasion, which on a subject of equal weight would be vicious and alien in correct and manly prose.

To me it has always seemed that all the resources of the language are open to a poet, but if he employs words or expressions with literary overtones, if his diction is out of the common way, he must make it justify itself. There are no rules except that of success, and out of the resources of a great living language what a poet deliberately picks for himself is not nearly so important as what, if he is attentive and receptive, the language will throw up unasked. It is not a storehouse waiting to be ransacked, but a moving and creative force continually adding to and renewing itself. It is, in a sense other than Goethe had in mind when he used the phrase, 'eine Sprache die für Dich dichtet und denkt.'* This is no process by which set habits, formulas and conventions take over, though this, too, happens when the poet is not able to hold his own or has nothing of his own to contribute. It is a process in which the poet has an integral part to play which demands the exercise of all his imagination and intelligence, but which demands also his participation and co-operation perhaps more than his direction and control. Pasternak, who must himself have experienced this in a well-known passage of the novel, pictures his poet hero. Yuri Zhivago suddenly coming to realize the nature of the process.

After a long interval Zhivago has the opportunity and the time to write poems again. He begins by making copies of poems he has already written, improving and changing them as he does so. Next he sets to work on old unfinished poems and having, as it were, 'warmed up' by this exercise he begins the composition of a new poem.

> After two or three stanzas, which came readily, and a few similes at which he himself was astonished, the work took possession of him and he experienced the onset of what is called inspiration. The correlation of forces organising the work of creation is then, as it were, turned upside down. The priority in this artistic process does not now rest with the man himself and the state of mind for which he is seeking expression, but with language, his means of expressing it. Language, the home and dwelling place of beauty and meaning, itself begins to think and speak for man and turns completely into music, not in the sense of external, audible sound, but in the sense of the impetus and power of its inward flow. Then, rolling in its might, like the current of a river, by the force of its own motion grinding the stones of its bed and turning the wheels of water-mills, the torrent of speech of its own accord, by the operation of laws of its own, creates in passing metre and

* A language which for you both speaks and thinks.

rhyme and thousands of other forms and formations even more important, but until this moment not discovered, not recognised and still nameless.

No one who has experienced this will ever talk of the composition of a poem, as some critics do, as though it were as deliberate an operation as cooking an omelet or laying bricks. What actually goes on, what forces are at work in the complex activity of composition is our next consideration.

9

Poems in the making

CARLYLE is said to have once made an enchanting remark about Tennyson: 'Alfred is always carrying a bit of chaos around with him and turning it into cosmos'. It is as surprising as it is enchanting, since Carlyle seems to have held no very high opinion of poets in general. But turning bits of chaos into cosmos is what every poet does every time he writes a poem. There is a sense in which each poem is a little world complete in itself, with its own logic, its own internal structure and its own emotional organization. What are the steps by which it comes into being, what forces are involved in the process and what parts do they play in it?

The first thing to notice is that there is no simple or single answer to these questions. Poets differ enormously in their methods of composition and in the degree to which they are aware of the process itself. They often differ greatly in the extent to which they plan and propose the course of a poem and exercise control and direction of that plan. Some poems seem to emerge, as it were, 'ready made'. I am not referring to the sort of reckless and inconsequent vomit of images which is sometimes offered—and published—as poetry today, but to finished and coherent poems which their authors confess to have taken them by surprise. Socrates' description of the phenomenon in the *Ion* is well known and shows that it was common enough in ancient Greece. Plato makes Socrates argue from the extreme position, that it is impossible to compose a true poem, even an epic, while the poet is in his right mind. He must abdicate all rational control, be dispossessed, or rather possessed, by the god or the Muse, who uses the poet as a means or conduit by which the divine being transmits poems in which the poet cannot claim to have much part in at all:

For the authors of those great poems which we admire, do not attain to excellence through rules of any art, but they utter their beautiful melodies of verse in a state of inspiration, and, as it were, *possessed* by a spirit not their own. Thus the composers of lyrical poetry create those admired songs of theirs in a state of divine insanity like the Corybantes who lose all control over their reason in the enthusiasm of the sacred dance; and, during this supernatural possession, are excited to the rhythm and harmony which they communicate to men.*

It is interesting to compare this account of 'inspiration' with that by Boris Pasternak at the end of the last chapter. It is interesting not so much because one supernatural agent appears to have replaced another, but because both writers so many thousand years apart, have come to the conclusion that in the actual process of composition, the poet, the man who writes or composes the poem, plays a comparatively minor part. I could add to this the testimony of a number of modern poets, persons not likely to be over-influenced by classical theories of divine inspiration. First of all I might invoke the author of *Also Sprach Zarathustra:*

If one had the smallest vestige of superstition in one, it would hardly be possible to set aside completely the idea that one is the mere incarnation, mouthpiece or medium of an almighty power. The idea of revelation in the sense that something suddenly becomes visible and audible with indescribable certainty and accuracy which profoundly convulses and upsets one describes simply a matter of fact. . . . Everything happens quite involuntarily, as if in a tempestuous outburst of freedom, of absoluteness, of power and divinity. The involuntariness of the figures and similes is the most remarkable thing: one loses all perception of what constitutes the figure and what constitutes the simile; everything seems to present itself as the readiest, the completest and the simplest means of expression. It actually seems, to use one of Zarathustra's own phrases, as if all things came unto one, and would fain be similes: 'Here do all things come winningly to thy talk and cajole thee, for they wish to ride upon thy back. On every simile dost thou ride here towards every truth . . . here all being desires to become words, here all being wishes to learn from you how to talk:'.

Nietzsche's attempts at poetry do not amount to much, but his *Zarathustra*, his masterwork, is more poem than prose

* Plato, *Ion* (Shelley's translation).

both in its imagery and its rhythms, so that we can add his testimony to that of the poets. Among English poets who have produced 'spontaneous' poems I can at the moment only recall Caedmon, Blake and Yeats, though there are doubtless many more. The only poem of Caedmon's that has survived, quoted in the Old English version of Bede's *History*, is a dream-poem. For the rest Bede's account is ambiguous. Caedmon, after this first spontaneous song, which he remembered on waking, was taken into the neighbouring monastery and there continued to compose poems with remarkable facility and speed on subjects, outlined to him by his teachers from sacred history

> and he retained in his memory whatever he learnt by hearing: and, like a clean animal, he ruminated and converted all into the sweetest music. And his song and his music were so delightful to hear, that even his teachers wrote down the words from his lips and learnt them.

This reference to Caedmon chewing the cud and converting it into fine poetry does sound like a spontaneous activity, especially as Caedmon had never composed poetry before, but it is not in Bede's original Latin text, where he simply says that Caedmon stored the bible stories in his memory and after meditating on them, turned them into melodious verse, which could mean no more than conscious and even painstaking composition. Still I like to think, with the Abbess Hild, that this was a case of genuine inspiration in the sense in which Socrates and Nietzsche describe it.

As for Blake, we have already mentioned his conviction that much of the Prophetic Books was taken down from dictation by angels. These were certainly not premeditated poems, but as poetry they are often involved, tediously prosy and in general though the matter may be inspired, the manner shows little sign of it. Blake fanciers will probably be horrified, but I find his later poems mainly interesting for the fact that genuine inspiration can result in very mediocre poetry. When Blake was *not* listening to his angels he was an inimitable poet.

Turning to Yeats, the monstrous *Variorum Edition* of his works, cluttering and messing the poet's considered final versions of his poems with all the rejected rubbish of his workshop, has at least a few things to be said in its favour. One is Yeats's own account on page 828 of how he came to write one of his most superb poems 'Leda and the Swan':

> I wrote 'Leda and the Swan' because the editor of a political review asked me for a poem. I thought, 'After the individualist demagogic movements founded by Hobbes and popularised by the Encyclopaedists and the French Revolution, we have a soil so exhausted that it cannot grow that crop again for centuries.' Then I thought, 'Nothing is now possible but some movement from above, preceded by some violent annunciation'. My fancy began to play with Leda and the Swan for metaphor, and I began this poem; but as I wrote, bird and lady took such possession of the scene that all politics went out of it and my friend tells me that his conservative readers would misunderstand the poem.

This was plainly a poem that insisted on writing itself, and Yeats was sensible enough to let it have its own way and to keep Hobbes, Diderot, Mirabeau and Co. completely out of it. I mention this instance because it illustrates the fact that there is no real difference in kind between the 'inspired' poem which emerges ready-made and the poem which is composed by the usual conscious processes but insists on taking its own course and ignoring the first intentions of the poet. Nor are these latter to be sharply distinguished from the sort of poem in which the subject proposed and the theme envisaged emerge more or less as planned, with the unforeseen enrichment provided by the dream-workers on the way. Good poems can emerge on all levels.

Nevertheless, because I have rarely experienced the onset of inspiration in the extreme sense in which Socrates and Nietzsche depict it, I am especially fascinated by accounts of those who have experienced it.

Goethe was one of them. One of his editors remarks:

> In the memoirs of his youth he recalls how he would frequently make poetry in a state approaching somnambulism or trance, sometimes waking and leaping out of bed in haste to scrawl down what had come to him before he forgot it as he often did. The lines Über allen gipfeln . . . (1780), probably the most famous of all German lyrics were suddenly scribbled on the wooden wall of a mountain hut. This gift of spontaneous poetry had not left him even in old age. The solemn and mysterious stanzas of 'Um Mitternacht ging ich' (he tells

us) emerged ready made into his mind on a moonlight winter night of 1818, unheralded and unexplained.

What this account does not make clear is that Goethe was not simply meditating in the moonlight but was taken by surprise on his return from a jolly evening party:

> Let me admit that on the stroke of midnight, in the most brilliant moonlight, returning from good, moderate, intelligent and agreeable company, I wrote down the poem on the spur of the moment, without my having had even the remotest inkling of it beforehand.

Another German poet Rainer Maria Rilke, in a similar testimony, gave much the same account of his famous *Sonnets to Orpheus*. Leishman's introduction to his translation of these remarkable poems quotes one of Rilke's letters:

> You mention the *Sonnets to Orpheus*: now and then they may show some lack of consideration for the reader. Even to me, in their rising up and imposing themselves upon me, they are perhaps the most mysterious, most enigmatic, dictation I have ever endured and performed; the whole first part was written down in a single breathless obedience, between the 2nd and the 5th of February 1922, and without one word being in doubt or requiring to be altered. And that at a time when I had got myself ready for another large work* and was already busy with it.

The great Russian poet Anna Akhmatova confessed to having written most of her largest and most elaborate work, *Poem without a Hero* in this way. In her prefatory remarks she says that the first part came to her one night on the 27th of December 1940 after sending a small fragment ahead during the previous autumn as a herald of its arrival. It came uncalled for and quite unexpected and that night she wrote two long sections of the work. This was during the siege of Leningrad and after her evacuation to Tashkent. 'Almost unexpectedly' she wrote another section, which was to become the third part of the poem, and made some basic interpolations in the first two parts already written down. In an interview some years later she remarked on the way the poem came to her.

> I did not write, as I usually do, crossing out and revising but exactly as though under dictation—as stanza after stanza laid

* *The Duino Elegies.*

itself down on the paper. And almost every stanza arrived already with its introduction, climax and conclusion.

This shows that a spontaneous poem need not come all in one piece and may be subject to a 'spontaneous' revision and continuation on later occasions. Indeed Akhmatova continued to work on the poem, to expand and edit it for many years afterwards.

These examples are enough, I think, to show that spontaneous poems, often of considerable length and complexity, do occur and perhaps more often than we imagine. A poet in the throes of composition is often so deeply immersed and absorbed that he is in a trance-like state and not always able to recall what went on, how much he composed and how much was delivered ready-made. We can conclude too, that whatever the source of such poems, the fact that they are spontaneous is no guarantee of excellence. It just happens that we notice the outstanding examples. Moreover we have already seen that all poetry has a spontaneous element in it, things that come unbidden, directions which the poem takes unexpectedly often to the surprise of its author and in addition what Pasternak calls 'forms and formations' (tysachi . . . form i obrazovanii) so new and singular that we have no names for them and recognize them only for the first time. It would seem reasonable to think of fully spontaneous poems not as exceptions or freaks of nature but as extreme instances and to posit a scale or gamut of instances up to the other extreme where the poet operates almost entirely consciously and to a preconceived plan. And poems at this end of the scale are not likely to be better or worse than those at the other. Nadyezhda Mandelshtam in her memoirs, after commenting on the fact that Mandelshtam himself was a 'spontaneous' poet, speaks scornfully of a poem which Pasternak wrote after he had been taken to hospital with a heart attack.

> In the work of any poet I can always distinguish between verse that wells up by itself from the depths of the mind and that which sets forth a preconceived idea. Akhmatova told me how she had heard Pasternak talk about being taken to hospital and what he though at the time. The poem he wrote later thus embodied his already existing account of the experience.

Nadyezhda Mandelshtam's criterion is too narrow. It would wipe out all narrative poetry, ballads on traditional themes, most satire, descriptive and deliberative poems. As a matter of fact, Pasternak's poem 'In Hospital' (V Bol'nitse), taking into account that it deals with the experience of a man who thinks he is probably going to die that night, is a clear, plain and moving poem dealing in its own terms with an emotion recollected in tranquillity. One does not interfere with this sort of experience even to the extent of leaving it to the back-room boys to turn it into something rich and strange, later to well up from the depths when it has been digested and transformed. Here is the poetry of pure experience and it has its own place, exists in its own right and is not touched by the fact that there are other kinds of poetry— other poetries in fact—a point on which I shall have more to say in a later chapter.

Even with the same sort of poetry the process may differ at different times. It is a mistake to divide the processes into two groups. Those that rise unforeseen and unbidden from the depths and those that are deliberately constructed at the level of consciousness. It is not as simple as that. A poem can be both premeditated and spontaneous and this can happen in several ways. For instance, I am reading a book, listening to music, recalling a dream or simply digging in the garden or shaving before the mirror. Something triggers an idea which I recognize by the curious excitement and expectancy that marks it off from other activities, as the material for a poem—then, in a flash, or growing in a few brief seconds, the whole plan and structure and 'feeling' of a possible poem presents itself. I may make a note or start at once to compose, but once the plan is there (itself a spontaneous and unpremeditated event) the rest may be perfectly deliberate and premeditated. Usually it is only partly so. As one works, more ideas, details, verbal adventures, images and rhythmical arrangements continue to well up and will often alter the original schema or replace the original projection of feeling with another and sometimes quite different one. Sometimes one becomes aware that more than one poem, or two variations on the original theme, are struggling for recognition and priority, or a new poem buds off from the original one. As the poem grows those parts that are already complete or roughed in, form patterns to which the new material can be fitted and developed. And in the midst of such routine carpenter's work a new image or a chance phrase or word, seen in passing when consulting a dictionary, will give new directions and overtones to what is almost complete. At other times one can deliberately propose a subject, or have it proposed, and in working at it quite as deliberately, discover its unguessed possibility, enter into its excitement and find a wealth of things welling up to fill out the framework, or, as Mallarmé describes it, 'crystallizing on the branch of metre.'

It has never been my fortune to be presented with a completely spontaneous poem and usually I work slowly, piecemeal, trying alternatives, fitting, improvising and often stopping because I cannot hit on the word or image which I feel is waiting just round the corner. Some poems, even quite short ones, are years a-growing. I have the feeling with some that I have to wait till I 'grow into them', just as I grow out of others and abandon them. But from time to time a poem does come almost ready made. It is consciously composed but in it everything seems to be at hand as I need it and I begin at the beginning and work straight through to the end. Once when I was working at the university in Melbourne, I began to have the unmistakeable feeling of 'having a poem coming on'. I put other things aside, but nothing would come and none of my already half-finished poems took fire when I tried to work over them. Finally I took a week off and borrowed a cottage by the sea, where I sat for three mortal days in front of a blank page without an idea in my head. At the end of the third day I decided to give up if nothing happened on the fourth. Next morning I sat down to my vigil and quite suddenly two poems appeared as if from nowhere and were composed in the course of a single morning, one straight after the other. The titles under which they were later published were 'Chorale' and 'William Butler Yeats'. That has been the nearest thing, in my experience, to having a poem emerge complete and ready made.

The sensation of 'having a poem coming on' in much the same sense as one speaks of feeling that one has a cold coming on, is one that I have had as long as I can remember and most other poets I know have said they experience it too. It has perhaps been best described in a poem by Anna Akhmatova called 'Creation' (Tvorchestvo) which I have ventured to translate:

> It is like this: a sort of lassitude;
> Unceasing in my ears, a striking clock,
> Far off a roll of thunder dies away.
> I seem to hear the groans and mournings of
> Voices imprisoned and unrecognised;
> The narrowing of a certain secret ring.
> Yet in this tingling, whispering abyss
> One all-subduing sound stands out so clear
> That round about unbroken stillness reigns,
> So that one hears the grass grow in the wood,
> Misery pace earth with his beggar's bag.
> But now already words are audible
> And signal chimes of rhythms light as air—
> Then I do begin to understand
> And, simply as they are dictated lines
> Lie down upon my snow-white writing pad.

In my own case the lassitude is usually followed and replaced by a feverish, and restless but quite undirected energy, a sort of probing and questing as though one were trying to pick up the scent. There is the same flood of disconnected images and illusion of sounds and the first hint of the emerging poem is often the disembodied rhythms which it will fill with words. The final stage with me, however, is the emergence of a single line or two. Akhmatova is plainly describing a spontaneous poem.

Another of the poems of which 'Creation' is the first and which she collected under the title of *Secrets of the Craft* (Tainy Remyesla) takes up a theme which Nietzsche refers to in his account of the 'inspiration' he experienced in writing *Zarathustra*. It is a not uncommon experience of poets that the objects and inhabitants of earth are pleading with the poet to give them expression, to make them live in words:

> There is much probably, that still desires
> Its celebration by this voice of mine:
> That which rumbles, beyond reach of words,
> Or underground in darkness grinds on stone,
> Or beats its way along through smoke.
> I have reckonings not yet resolved

With flame and with water and with wind . . .
That is why for me my drowsings
All of a sudden fling such gates wide open
And carry me beyond the morning star.

When I first read the original of this I recalled having the same odd feeling from time to time and having embodied it in a poem based on a hint from Baudelaire about the desire of the wine for the apotheosis of being drunk by man:

All things solicit the poet for his art
To change dumb being into sentient wine;
Flowers turn their faces, stones implore his feet.
Drunk with those lives he reels towards the sign
Where, in his turn, the secular paraclete
Cries: Drink, engulf me, let me feel my heart.

This is not merely a pretty fancy. It is a reflection of what Keats called negative capability, which he noted as the most important characteristic of a poet:

As to the Poetical Character itself . . . it is not itself—it has no character—it enjoys light and shade; it lives in gusto, be it foul or fair, high or low, rich or poor, mean or elevated—it has as much delight in conceiving an Iago as an Imogen . . . a poet is the most unpoetical of anything in existence because he has no identity—he is continually in for—and filling some other Body—the sun, the moon, the sea and men and women who are creatures of impulse, are poetical and have about them an unchanging attribute—the poet has none: no identity.

Important as this insight into the poet's relation to the external world may be, there is an even more important kind of negative capability which he must encourage in himself in relation to his *internal* world, or that part of it which is concerned with the making of poems. It is here that the accounts of spontaneous poems are particularly important, because they stress that element in the composition of a poem in which the poet realizes that he is only a participant in a team of forces all contributing to the total composition. In this he may be aware of the difference between his position and that of other artists, who usually assume that they are firmly in the saddle; but, on the other hand, he knows that he is not in the position of some miserable script-writer for Elstree or Hollywood, treated as a mere producer of raw material for the eventual film. He knows that all these other

H

forces are part of himself and depend on him as much as he on them—even the language, as Pasternak and Goethe describe it, is only a living force insomuch as he has given it the life that seems to take over so imperiously at times.

Among various attempts as describing the *dramatis personae* of this team, I can think of none so clearly conceived as that in Anna Akhmatova's *Secrets of the Craft*. These poems belong to different periods in the poet's life and do not represent a planned or even a complete view. The characters involved in the making of a poem may not comprise the complete cast and in any case they are only 'characters' in a mythological sense, like the allegorical characters in a Courtly Love dream poem, or the very suspect entities to which Freudian psychology gave a local habitation and a name at the end of the last century. Let us call them 'Working Fictions' and think of them in terms of a Platonic myth. As Plato pointed out there are some problems which we cannot, at our particular stage of knowledge, deal with in scientific or even pragmatically descriptive terms. All we can do is to embody what we know, or suspect to be the case, in a fable. The characters in this fable are not real independent agents, any more than an Idleness, Mirth, Bialacoil, Danger, Franchise, Courtesy and the rest in the love allegory of the *Romaunt of the Rose* or Ego, Super-ego, Unc and Id in the knock-about Freudian myth. They represent forces at work in my own mind which contribute in one way or another to the making of a poem. There is first of all the conscious poet-craftsman who has to help the poem to grow, keep it coherent and control extravagance and irrelevance to which the dream-workers are only too prone. This Akhmatova calls the Poet and in a poem with this title acknowledges the hard and exacting work that his rôle involves

> Just think! it is work as well
> This carefree life:
> To overhear something in music
> And pass it off in jest as one's own.
> And as one sets down some gay scherzo
> In some sort of lines or other
> To swear that the wretched heart
> Groans so among glittering fields.

The stress here is on the effort to 'overhear' and translate rather than deliberately to direct and invent. The hard work, then tension, arises because letting the sub-conscious forces have their way, and acting as 'manager' and arbiter of the poem, pull in opposite directions much of the time.

Among these sub-conscious, or as I should prefer to call them, subliminal forces which so far I have simply lumped together as the Dream-Team, Akhmatova makes clear distinctions. Among these are the voices of the world engaging the poet to speak for them. These, as it were, operate by attracting attention, involving the poet in their existence and provoking a desire to give them expression in a poem. I have already mentioned the poem in which she confesses debts still unfulfilled to the natural world. In another she repudiates the kind of poem which is planned in advance, or follows a fixed form like the ode or the sonnet, and goes on to describe how odd objects in the natural world trigger off poems. Such poems, unlike spontaneous poems, are consciously composed but not necessarily consciously conceived and planned.

> I have no use for odes in full parade
> Nor elegies with their embellished charm;
> For me in verse things should not fall too pat
>   As folk would have them be.
> If you but knew out of what sort of litter
> Poems arise and with no sense of shame!
> Like yellow dandelions beside a fence,
>   Like burdocks and like goose-foot.
> A shout of anger, the fresh smell of tar,
> Mysterious patch of mould upon a wall . . .
> Forthwith a verse rings out, fervent and tender
>   To your delight and mine.

To this sense of the whole natural world as an active participant in the initiation and the growth of a poem—we could call this member of the cast Nature—she added another whom we could call Humanity, a natural urge to speak for and in the voice of one's fellow-beings. In the dedication of *Poem without a Hero* to her friends and fellow citizens who perished in the terrible siege of Leningrad she said:

> I hear their voices and remember them when I read the poem aloud and this secret chorus has always been for me a justification of the work.

But in conversation with her friend Lydia Chukovskaya she went further, saying,

> It is a strange piece, very strange. I have always written my poems myself. But well, with the *Poem* it was different. I wrote down the whole thing as if a member of a group, together with the others as though I were being prompted.

I cannot fail to remember that Wordsworth, a poet so different and so distant in time and place from Akhmatova, recorded the same two external influences in his 'Lines written a Few Miles above Tintern Abbey' (1798). He records, indeed something that Akhmatova took for granted, the intense force with which the natural world importunes the poet.

> The sounding cataract
> Haunted me like a passion: the tall rock
> The mountain and the deep and gloomy wood,
> Their colours and their odours were to me
> An appetite: a feeling and a love
> That had no need of a remoter charm,
> By thought supplied, or any interest
> Unborrowed from the eye

Cataract, mountain, gloomy wood and the rest of course had no interest in young Wordsworth, but the images of these things in his mind became living thoughts demanding their translation into language.

Wordsworth goes on to Akhmatova's second character, the human, speaking through the poet.

> That time is past
>
> . . .
>
> For I have learned
> To look on nature not as in the hour
> Of thoughtless youth, but hearing often times
> The still, sad music of humanity,

This is the situation of the poet: the whole natural world, the whole form and pressure of his society absorbs and then demands his attention and his giving them a voice. If this was all that poetry demanded it would be an important but minor physiological and psychological part of the machinery of adjustment. But it is responding to these voices which opens gates of discovery that carry the poet—as Akhmatova says—beyond the morning star.

Akhmatova identifies another of these shaping forces in the making of a poem as the audience to whom the poem is addressed. This is, of course, not any actual audience but the one the poet has in mind when he writes the poem. This is a part of his mind and determines the way the poem is written it is one of the persons in the team. In a poem called 'The Reader' ('chitatyel') the first two stanzas picture the intolerable situation of the poet who tries to communicate directly with his contemporaries. He stands as though in the glare of limelight separated from them on a stage and hopelessly theatrical. Then she pictures the real reader who has a part in the production of poems. He is a mystery, like a treasure buried in the earth, he never reveals himself but his felt presence helps to evoke all that nature hides from us and

> Those unknown eyes
> Talk to me until the light [of dawn]
> They reproach me for this or that,
> About this or that they agree with me.
> So the dumb confession flows on,
> A blissful fervour of conversation.
> Our century on this earth flows swiftly
> And its appointed circle is tight,
> But he is changeless and everlasting,
> The poet's unknown friend.

Two other great poets of the period, her friends Pasternak and Mandelshtam, held similar views on this point. In a perceptive essay about the reader to whom a poet addresses his poem, 'About the Interlocutor' (O Sobyesyednike) Mandelshtam dismisses the poet who addresses himself to a specific contemporary audience as a mere *littérateur* lecturing to his age from a position of superiority. The true, the providential interlocutor is always unknown and unspecified. The poet writes for him like someone who encloses a message in a bottle and throws it into the sea in hope that somewhere, someday a reader will pick it up and understand. Pasternak in his autobiographical work, *Safe Conduct*, speaks of the danger of the specific contemporary audience 'taking over' the poet so that he writes in response to their demands on him and not from the depths of himself:

The time comes when suddenly into the one degenerating dilating heart [of the poet], there pour all the responses which already and for a long time past have been coming from other hearts in answer to the beating of this principal one, which continues to pulse strongly, to think and to wish to live. So that as they multiply all the time, they beat faster till they suddenly keep pace and coincide with the shudders of the principal heart; they begin to live as one life with him and henceforth keep the same beat.

When this happens, says Pasternak, Pushkin, even Pushkin, is no longer his own man, he is 'everybody's Pushkin'.

I find myself very much in sympathy with such views. I am often asked in the course of interviews: 'What audience do you have in mind when you are writing a poem'? and I can only answer: 'None and no one in particular'. I say this not because it is really true but because it is too difficult to explain that mostly I have a perfectly definite reader in view, a reader who is more or less formulated or demanded by the poem, a reader who would like, fully comprehend and completely enter into this particular poem. But if I try to explain this to a busy journalist, I can see him make a mental note: 'Does not know who he is talking to' and he breaks into my explanation and changes the subject. But I know that without this unknown yet quite definite interlocutor—a good word, a better word than 'audience' or 'reader' because I always have a feeling that a poem is personal conversation—I should be very much at a loss. It is the sense of his presence that helps me to make all sorts of minute decisions on which the 'tone' of the poem depends. It is he who allows me now to be easy and slacken rein, now to relax high seriousness and now to modulate to another mood or mode, to choose one word or image and reject another, to expand here and concentrate there. The interlocutor is my ombudsman in the debates that constantly arise between the way I want the poem to go and the way the poem seems bent on pursuing.

I share, too, the sense of dangers to the free development of some poems, if one is too conscious of an audience that needs to be placated, cajoled, entreated or simply pleased on their own terms. And yet I cannot help feeling that a poet who does not care whether he communicates or not, who does not care if he is wilful and arbitrary, or just plain incomprehensible, runs even greater risks. Of course, one has to remember that these three Russian poets, at the time they wrote, were not simply weaving literary theories. Their backs were to the wall, they were defending themselves against the pressure, an almost intolerable pressure, to conform, to write poems addressed to Soviet readers, conveying party views of proper subjects and party views of proper treatments on party lines. They were in retreat to the last stronghold of the Muses—and in the end they won by simply refusing to compromise. Those who gave in to political and social pressures and wrote to order for a Soviet audience indeed became mere littérateurs, even Mayakovsky, who was a poet of real genius. They will be forgotten. Pasternak, Akhmatova, Tsvetaeva and Mandelshtam are gradually being recognised, even in official literary circles in Russia, as the real poets of the period.

Another consideration may have led them to the doctrine of the unknown interlocutor and that is the fact that their poetry was almost entirely lyric. It is as hard to believe that the great narrative, dramatic and philosophic poems of the past were not addressed to a quite specific contemporary audience as it is to deny that they were great poetry for this reason. We should have to deny that a great deal of love poetry, religious poetry, verse epistles and satire were true poems if the criterion were to be rigidly or crassly applied.

Finally among the personae engaged in Akhmatova's team there is the Muse, whom she addressed or about whom she speaks in a number of poems. The Muse is the bestower of the divine gift of poetry, of inspiration which she sometimes grants and at other times withholds. The poet must wait for her coming and until she appears all the other participants in the creative process are helpless to proceed. The Muse initiates; the Muse guides and controls. A comparison of the various poems in this group suggests that the Muse is not simply a literary convention and that she is a personal tutelary figure rather than those general arbiters and instigators of literary works represented by the Muses of the classical tradition. The Muse is a real person, a sort of *alter ego*, a part of the poet's make-up but distinguished from the person who practises the craft and lives out the daily life of experience through which the subjects of poetry and the unknown reader play their parts in the composition of poems. The Muse, however, though personal to each poet, is also one and the same for all poets and so perhaps represents the tradition. In many of the poems Akhmatova speaks of the Muse as a sister or a close companion, but in a poem written in 1924 she appears as a severe and remote mentor to whom the poet is in tutelage.

> When at night I await her coming,
> Life, so it seems, hangs on a single thread.
> What is honour, what is youth, what is freedom then
> In the presence of this mild guest, pipe in hand?
> And see, she enters, turning back her veil,
> Taking a long look, she considers me.
> I say to her, 'Was it you, then, dictated
> To Dante the pages of *Hell*?' She answers,
>
> 'It was I.'

In my own experience, just as I have rarely had the experience of a 'dictated' poem, so on the other hand, I have always had a strong feeling of a mentor which I can vaguely associate with the voice of those parts of the tradition to which I feel allegiance, translated into the sense of an *alter ego*, without whose presence the poem, however clearly I conceive its general outline, cannot get under way. Others, I think, have felt it too. Milton's invocation to the 'Heav'nly Muse' may be a literary device but his following prayer to the Holy Spirit,

> . . . what in me is dark
> Illumine, what is low raise and support;
> That to the heighth of this great Argument
> I may assert Eternal Providence,

is not and a poet as different from Milton as it is possible to imagine apparently felt at least that a second person was involved in the making of poetry. At the age of sixteen Rimbaud wrote to his former teacher on account of his latest discovery:

> Je me suis reconnu poète. Ce n'est pas du tout ma faute. C'est faux de dire: Je pense. On devrait dire: On me pense . . . Je est un autre.*

Two days later he wrote another letter in which he said:

> Je est un autre. Si le cuivre s'eveille clairon, il n'y a rien de sa faute. Cela m'est evident: j:assiste à l'éclosion de ma pensée: je

---

* I have discovered that I am a poet. It is not at all my fault. It is false to say: I think. One should say: I am being thought . . . 'I' is someone else.

la regarde, je l'écoute: je lance un coup d'archet: la symphonie
fait son remuement dans les profondeurs ou vient d'un bond
sur la scène.*

At the time he wrote this Rimbaud was obviously doing
more than acting as a spectator, while someone else com-
posed the poems. They bear all the marks of co-operative and
craftsman-like composition, but his later work in *Les Illu-
minations* and *Une Saison en Enfer* show only too clearly the
degeneration of a talent that occurs where the 'poet', in Akh-
matova's sense, withdraws from the team—as the surrealist
poetry of half a century later was to demonstrate. At least
Rimbaud was aware of more than one agent in the process,
but he had chosen the wrong way to split the poetic per-
sonality.

I have often wondered what W. B. Yeats meant by his
theory of the mask as essential to poetry or the poet. I have
never read a satisfactory explanation and I suspect that Yeats
himself never really knew. As so often happens in this twi-
light world where a poet tries to look inward at his own pro-
cesses of composition, the best he can do is tell the thing
in the form of a rather ambiguous myth, which is, all I am
trying to do here. For the most part Yeats seems to be talking
about the need to create an artificial or consciously con-
structed 'anti-self', or a series of dramatic persons who act in
this way—and no doubt this is another way to approach the
problem of the forces involved in composition, though for
the most part these characters, as Yeats describes them are
not concerned with composition. When he says in *Autobio-
graphies,*

> . . . as I look backward upon my own writing, I take pleasure
> alone in those verses where it seems to me I have found some-
> thing hard and cold, some articulation of the Image, which is
> the opposite of all that I am in my daily life.

there is at least a recognition that there has been another
persona at work and that composition for Yeats was as much
a matter of discovery as of co-operative craft-work.

It remains to ask whether in this shadowy crowd some

---

* 'I' is someone else. If brass wakes to find itself a trumpet, it is not to blame
for that at all. To me this is obvious: I witness the unfolding of my
thought, I watch it and listen to it: I make a stroke with the bow: the
symphony begins to stir in the depths or leaps upon the stage.

have not been identified by the poets whose witness I have quoted. I can only think of two: they are both apt to be deleterious and both are extremely active in contemporary poetry: they are the voices, sometimes sounding in unison, of contemporary poetic theories and contemporary fashionable practice. But these can best be dealt with in a later chapter.

It is best not to try to be too explicit in these matters. Many other poets would suggest other fables and there would probably be truth in all of them. For myself I am not concerned to try to elicit from such fables anything like a precise psychological theory. A poet is wise to keep a large measure of that negative capability of which Keats wrote,

> When man is capable of being in uncertainties, Mysteries, doubts, without any irritable reaching after fact and reason.

This region of the poet's mind is where the roots are working and feeding; pulling them up to see how they do it buys knowledge perhaps at the expense of poetry itself.

10

How Poems Grow

THE last chapter was largely concerned with the agents at work in the growth of a poem and with the testimony of other poets. Very few poets have given any account of the way actual poems grow and the critics who try to reconstruct the process from drafts and chance remarks by the authors are, as I shall show, often apt to be wildly astray. So in dealing with this topic I shall draw in the main from my own recollection and observation.

It is clear that no single account of how poems grow will fit all cases. No doubt all the elements and agents at work are present in some degree, but it is obvious that a long narrative poem like *Troilus and Criseyde*, or the *Lusiads* of Camoens, both of which have their main lines laid down beforehand, the one in legend, the other in history, cannot be left to material 'welling up from the depths', nor can a novel in verse like *Eugene Onegin* or Byron's *Don Juan*. These, like a long philosophic poem such as the *De Rerum Natura*, have to be planned and their general architecture determined in advance. The poet has to be able to take charge to much greater extent. The longest poem I have ever composed was a mock epic, *Dunciad Minor* and it was certainly, like all mock epics, consciously based on previous models and planned carefully in advance of the writing. Yet I was surprised to find that this planning and this conscious approach did not at all inhibit the contribution and the co-operation of the other agents below or behind the level of conscious proposal and disposal. On the contrary, during the writing of the poem I was constantly bombarded with ideas, suggestions, images and echoes, to the point where I could hardly cope with the flow. The plan itself seemed to stimulate and engender them. The other agents were so enthusiastic to help that they flooded me with suggestions and ideas twenty-four hours a day. I came to the conclusion that the modern fear of conscious planning in poetry is largely due to the fact that so many of the great forms have fallen into disuse. Nobody actually knows what it was like to write a mock epic or an epyllion, let alone an epic itself. And this ignorance is reflected in the inadequate theories about poetry to be discussed in the next chapter.

What I am concerned with in this chapter is a certain school of criticism which has become popular in recent years that interprets a poem in the light of all the material which went into the making of it. This often results in a serious distortion of the poem and in some cases may be based on a false notion of the way the poem grew. I take as examples of this sort of inflation of a poem the treatment of Yeats's 'Leda and the Swan', by Giorgio Melchiori in *The Whole Mystery of Art* and by T. R. Henn in *The Lonely Tower*. All Yeat's reading and all the pictures he is known to have looked at and all his other works are ransacked for evidence. Henn has conveniently summarized Melchiori and added comments of his own when talking of the pictures and symbols he thinks are involved in the poem. Here is the result:

> Melchiori has developed at length the intricate background of the poem: how Pater had discussed the parallel between Helen and St Anne, and how the complexities include Madame Blavatsky's *The Secret Doctrine,* the relationship to an illustration of Blake's 'Jerusalem', the two-fold debt to Spenser, Shelley's translation of the 'Homeric' Hymn to the Dioscuri, Gogarty's 'An Offering of Swans,' Gustave Moreau's *Leda.* He has discussed in detail all (I think), the possible sources, including some of the suggestions which I had made in the first edition of this book. To this it would be presumptuous to add: except to note that among the Ricketts drawings is the scene of the winged angel in a narrow cell, the terrified half-naked girl clasping his feet: that a Cretan coin shows the union of the dove ('Dove or Swan') with Dictynna, the Cretan Diana, and the Swan may be a phallic symbol. Raymond Lister has drawn my attention to the possible relevance of the woman-swan figure in Plate 11 of 'Jerusalem'. But since Melchiori's book was published a further dimension has been given by Wind, who points out the connection of Leda with Death, and confirms the link with Michelangelo's *Night.* Through this there

is the connection with the Neo-Platonic conception of the 'Eros funèbre' and the kiss of death.

The poem is perhaps the test case for the extent to which we may, if we wish, pursue meanings in depth. Let us take the poem first in its simplicity.

Two Annunciations form a pattern in history: Leda and the Virgin. The Virgin is linked, mistakenly, to St Anne, via Pater's Essay. Both events concern the union of godhead and woman. Both produce momentous births. The eggs of Leda give rise to the fall of Troy; from them emerge the legend of two destined women Helen and Clytemnestra. Helen has long been a personal symbol for Maude Gonne. The swans are archetypal, everywhere; in Spenser, emblems, paintings, Celtic myth, and concretely on the lakes at Coole. The swan stands for power, phallic strength, purity, spirit and spirits (as all white birds), fidelity; fire and air (as the dove); the ineffable Godhead. In the act of congress the 'loosening thighs' and the 'white rush' are antithetical aspects. Into the softness and whiteness is concentrated all the sensuality of touch. The outcome of the union is further history or myth, pagan or Christian, Love and War. But what of the woman? Yeats speculates continually on the emotions of woman in such a crisis. Did Leda or Mary by that act become half or wholly divine? Did a god share with beast the lassitude that overcomes all animals, save only the lion and the cock? *Shudder* is of the sexual act, the moment of orgasm, as all husbandmen know; but it is also anticipation in fear.

The verbal tensions are everywhere. The 'white rush' is perhaps not only from Spenser, but the wind of Pentecost. The *beating* heart is the assurance of incarnation, not of the immaterial or ghostly. The 'dark webs' (which replaced the earlier, and ridiculous, 'webbed toes'), give a paradox of bleak cold to cut across the finger associations of the sensual caress. Behind the poem, its phonetic subtlety, its changes of speed, what do the depth references add? Many pictures, coins, emblems, confirm the centrality of the myth. Two world events converge, compress, in a paradox of cosmic implications, in a synthesis of virility, sensuality, and of the traditional and necessary domination. To embrace the monstrous fact strains all imagination; Semele, Danaë, the faintly comic Europa are thin or insignificant by comparison.

Behind again (but I think faintly) may be the Leda-Leto equation, the ironic questioning of the permanence of the supreme sexual act, the relation of male to female, god to

mortal, god to woman. Dove or Swan; and behind them stand-
ing lonely and a little sardonically, the image of the White
Heron.

One can only say that all this farrago of sources, symbols and
cross-reference *may* be relevant. They may quite possibly
have been in the poet's mind, or operating below the surface
of awareness, as the conscious and unconscious fragments of
Coleridge's reading were in the background and combined
to produce 'The Ancient Mariner'. But with Coleridge Pro-
fessor Lowes has been able to show that the material, how-
ever changed and transfigured, is really there in the poem.
It can be identified. Whether the identification adds any-
thing to the understanding or enjoyment of the poem, is
another question. I am inclined to think not. *The Road to
Xanadu* does not illuminate 'The Ancient Mariner'; its in-
terest lies in its illumination of the poet's mind, of the crea-
tive imagination at work. But the materials brought forward
by Messrs Melchiori and Henn, while they may equally illu-
minate the workings of the poet's mind, have, in fact, very
little to do with the poem in question at all. Practically none
of it is *in the poem*. Helen and St Anne, Madame Blavatsky's
Secret Doctrine and Blake's *Jerusalem*, The Homeric Hymn
and the Dioscuri, Gogarty's poem and Moreau's painting,
Rickett's drawing and the Cretan coin, Leda as Leto, Michel-
angelo's statue of Night on the Medici tombs, the funerary
Eros, the Annunciation to the Virgin Mary, Spenser's swans
and the Lake at Coole and so on and so on, to the White
Heron. They may, as I say, have been in the mind of Yeats
when he wrote the poem, but they are not in the poem it-
self even by the faintest hint or allusion. What *is* in the
poem is an account of the legend of Leda's possession by
Zeus in the shape of a swan, a reference to the war of Troy
which was occasioned by the rape of Helen one of the off-
spring of this mating, and a surmise or question as to
whether Leda might not have had a prophetic intuition of
these consequences of the mating under the influence of the
divine possession. To import all the junk assembled by the
two critics is not to illuminate the poem in the least. On the
contrary it distorts it and ruins its essentially simple and
profound treatment of the legend in its own terms. We recall,
with amusement, that this erudite pair of literary dustmen

has overlooked the fact that in 'Leda and the Swan' Yeats set out to write a *political* poem, with Hobbes, the Encyclopaedists and the French Revolution in the foreground and the irruption of the divine and Leda's prevision of the war of Troy as an illustrative image. Surely, under the critics' own procedure, these 'sources' should have had a place with the rest of the lumber. They have ignored Yeats's own account of how the poem grew and replaced it by fictions of their own.

They were on dangerous ground in any case. Poems differ enormously in the changes that take place between the first conception and their final form. To illustrate this to a lecture audience, I once took two poems of my own whose origins I could well remember, set them side by side and tried to imagine a sources-and-allusion type of critic dealing with them to his own satisfaction. As poems one seemed to me about as good as the other, but they had come into existence in very different ways indeed. The first was a poem in memory of a favorite poet, Osip Mandelshtam, a victim of the Stalin Terror in 1938. It is an imaginary account of his death, which seems to have occurred in a staging camp near Vladivostok on his way to the forced labour camps of the Kolyma. During the two years before I wrote the poem I had been reading Mandelshtam's verse and his critical prose with growing interest and pleasure and had written two long articles on certain of his poems in the volume he published in 1922 under the title of *Tristia*. During the same period I had read all I could about the poet in contemporary memoirs and what suggested the poem in the first instance was the accounts of Mandelshtam's last days which his wife managed to collect from survivors over the next few years. The whole idea of the poem occurred to me quite consciously and quickly and, as I now see from successive drafts, the composition followed the original plan except for a change of title, a change from the old Rhyme Royal stanza in which I began it to a six-line stanza, in which I feel more at home, and the dropping of a first stanza, after the poem was completed, at the suggestion of a fellow poet. Originally called 'The Death of the Poet', it was published under the title, 'In Memoriam O.E.M., December 1938.'

> They marched in the first snow; the angry wind
> Tore at his rags; they had given him a spade

To dig a hole in Asia, but he stood
Listening strangely alert and staring blind.
'My mad Aonides have come,' he said;
'Their singing is this sobbing of my blood.'

He had reached that final moment when the frames
Of time and space reel inwards and collapse.
Floating on air, granite Petropolis,
Just as he had foretold, went up in flames
—or was it Ilium ablaze, perhaps?—
And surely that undaunted head was his.

Clairvoyant Cassandra—in Troy or in Tashkent?
The images fused and wavered to confuse
Yelabuga with stony Troezene;
A black sun raging in the firmament
Half showed Marina choking in the noose,
Half Phaedra in her death-throes, hapless queen.

A guard's voice crashed through with a harsh command;
He set the spade's edge in the frozen ground
And saw the pebbles through his transparent boot,
The wooden haft through his translucent hand
Persephone's bees with a sad murmuring sound
Swarmed from a cavern that opened underfoot.

And throwing back his head, he laughed aloud
And cupped his hands in the archaic pose
Of suppliants bringing offerings to a tomb,
Saying: 'Lady of the dark star and the bright cloud,
Out of the house of exile, at this close,
I have learned at last the art of coming home'.

'I come, my sister, as Pindar came,' he said,
Because he had not yet made you any song,
To celebrate your divinity with one
In which I praise the labours of the dead.
Take from my palms gifts which to you belong:
A little honey and a little sun!'

The industrious commentator should have little trouble
with this poem. All its references except one are to be found
quite easily in the background of reading I have indicated
and were brought into the poem quite consciously. The
'mad Aonides' (the Muses) are taken from a reference in
one of Mandelshtam's poems and from the memoirs of the
poet Irina Odoyevtseva, who happened on Mandelshtam

composing this very poem and was questioned by the poet about a line from Pushkin (or so he thought),

The sobbing of the mad Aonides

the reference to Petropolis (Petrograd/Leningrad) is to another poem of Mandelshtam's in which he prophetically anticipated the city's destruction during its nine hundred days' siege by the Germans. Cassandra's prophecy of the fall of Troy is linked with his friend, the poet Anna Akhmatova, whom he addressed in a poem as Cassandra and who was evacuated to Tashkent during the same siege. In the same way the fate of another close friend, the poet Marina Tsvetaeva, who was sent at the same time to the city of Yelabuga and there hanged herself in despair, is equated with the fate of Phaedra in 'stony Troezene'—a phrase taken from a fragmentary poem about Phaedra in Mandelshtam's *Tristia*—who hanged herself in despair after failing to win the love of her stepson Hippolytus. The transparent boot and hand take their significance from the fact that the three poems by Mandelshtam that I had translated and written a commentary on, all deal with the classical world of the dead, where everything is 'transparent'. In the third of these poems the wild bees of Persephone which inhabit the underworld also represent the Muses. The transition from this to the reference to Pausanias's story about Pindar and the wild bees and Persephone would be an easy one to follow since I had retold the story in another poem in the same volume.* 'I have learned at last the art of coming home' and 'take from my palms . . . a little honey and a little sun' are echoes of actual lines in poems by Mandelshtam. Everything, as you might say, is straightforward and above-board. Apart from Mandelshtam's theory that the civilisation of ancient Greece was reviving in the Russia of his day, a theory the reader is supposed to know and take for granted as background, everything I have mentioned among the sources of the poem is actually present in the poem and would not need mention but for the fact that English speaking readers are likely to be unfamiliar with a background which would need no comment for Russian readers. The poem was written straight through from beginning to end as it stands in

---

* 'The Wild Bees', *A Late Picking*, p. 81.

J

the final version. Any critic who made this assumption would be quite right, though I do not know what good it would do him.

It would certainly do him no good at all to make the same assumptions about the second poem, 'The School of Night'. This is a very different kettle of fish. But I shall say no more about it until the reader has been able to judge what he can deduce about its composition from the text itself.

The School of Night

What did I study in your School of Night?
When your mouth's first unfathomable yes
Opened your body to be my book, I read
My answers there and learned the spell aright,
Yet, though I searched and searched, could never guess
What spirits it raised nor where their questions led.

Those others, familiar tenants of your sleep,
The whisperers, the grave somnambulists
Whose eyes turn in to scrutinize their woe,
The giant who broods above the nightmare steep,
That sleeping girl, shuddering, with clenched fists,
A vampire baby suckling at her toe,

They taught me most. The scholar held his pen
And watched his blood drip thickly on the page
To form a text in unknown characters
Which, as I scanned them, changed and changed again:
The lines grew bars, the bars a Delphic cage
And I the captive of his magic verse.

But then I woke and naked in my bed
The words made flesh slept, head upon my breast;
The bed rode down the darkness like a stream;
Stars I had never seen danced overhead.
'A blind man's fingers read love's body best:
Read all of me!' you murmured in your dream,

'Read me, my darling, translate me to your tongue,
That strange Man-language which you know by heart;
Set my words to your music as they fall;
Soon, soon, my love! The night will not be long;
With dawn the images of sleep depart
And its dark wisdom fades beyond recall.'

Here I stand groping about the shores of light
Too dazzled to read that fading palimpsest;

Faint as whisper that archaic hand
Recalls some echo from your school of night
And dead sea scrolls that were my heart attest
How once I visited your holy land.

One can imagine a critic of Giorgio Melchiori's kidney studying this poem in the light of the sort of information about the ideas, the reading and the contacts with works of art of its author which he had amassed, as in the case of W. B. Yeats's 'Leda and the Swan'. In that case Melchiori developed an elaborate theory of mystical-historical symbolism, in which Leda's coupling with swan and the birth of Helen are shown to be prototypes of the Virgin Mary impregnated by the Holy Dove, the Paraclete, and of the birth of Christ. It is a theory developed over more than a hundred pages and as we have seen, the poem itself gives not the slightest warrant for it. I am going to improve on the method so that my imaginary source-hound at least builds his theory on things that are actually *in* the poem.

He assumes to start with that the poem was composed straight through from beginning to end. I have been dead for some years, so that he has access to my papers, has read all I have published and can tell you most of the books I have read, the pictures I have looked at and the places I have visited. There is practically nothing he does not know—except how the poem in question came into being.

The first clue he hits on is the title which, as it is repeated in the first stanza, he assumes to have been contemporaneous with the composition of the poem. He knows of my interest in Marlowe (at least two published essays and an unpublished attempt at restoration of the original text of Dr Faustus). He has evidence that I have read Muriel Bradbrook's study, *The School of Night*, about the circle of scientists and literary men who gathered round Sir Walter Raleigh and engaged in daring and unorthodox speculation and were accused by contemporaries of atheism and of practising necromancy and other black arts. He notes the reference to the magic book in the first stanza and links it at once with Dr Faustus selling his soul to the devil for a book of magic spells. He then turns to Shakespeare's *Love's Labour's Lost,* from which the phrase 'the school of night' is taken

> Black is the badge of hell
> The hue of dungeons and the school of night:
> And beauty's crest becomes the heavens well.*

This is almost certainly a reference to the group who gathered round Raleigh and in the same scene Berowne in a long speech compares women to books, which are the basic source of all knowledge:

> From women's eyes this doctrine I derive
> They sparkle still the true Promethean fire,
> They are the books, the Arts, the Academes
> That show, contain, and nourish all the world.
> Else none at all in aught proves excellent.

By this time our researcher is sure he is on the right track. Looking down the page he notes the scholar with his own blood dripping from his pen. Yes, of course, this must be the speaker in the poem, who is an academic as well as a poet, in the character of Dr Faustus signing his bond with the Devil—only here the power of darkness is a woman. But what woman? Well the 'Delphic cage' is surely the clue. Delphi was the main seat of the god of song, Apollo and of the mysterious Sybil who uttered his prophecies in even more mysterious verse. The scholar having made his compact with the powers of love and night, finds his commentary turning to poetry and the bond he has signed with them holds him captive. At this point our critic supports this identification by an account of my own visit to Delphi which I put down in one of my notebooks. It confirms the deep significance which Delphi had for me.

The following stanza takes us back to Marlowe and the Raleigh circle. It was said that one of them, the brilliant mathematician and astronomer Thomas Harriot, taught younger members to mock the Scriptures, to make fun of the articles of the Christian faith, such as the immortality of the soul, and to spell the name of God backwards. Marlowe's Faustus, of course, as part of his pact with the Devil has to renounce Christianity. This theme is clearly in the background of the renunciation of Christianity—for the black magic of love is indicated where the word is made flesh, but as the body of a naked woman, not that of the crucified Christ. Their bed becomes a boat and sets out on the journey

* Act IV, scene III.

of occult enlightenment for now the scholar-lover-poet is able to read the book of her body and translate its secret wisdom into human language. The reference to the stars not seen before reminds the reader that Harriot, one of the leading astronomers of the day and inventor of the telescope at the same time as Galileo, was probably the leader of the School of Night and their daring adventure towards new knowledge.

However at this point the speaker is represented as blind, reading the book of his mistress's body with his fingers and the reference appears to be to the prophet and seer Tiresias, who was visited with blindness for seeing a goddess naked but compensated with the gift of prophecy. So the character of seer is now added to those of scholar, poet and lover and the sleeper awakens a complete adept.

It would be convenient here to refer to an early poem of mine on the subject of Tiresias, in which he was driven blind as a result of seeing the mating of Jupiter and Juno. The poem has not survived but we can imagine it to have been recovered by later scholarship. It would be quite in line with the sort of criticism we are imagining, for the writer to import this into the poem to strengthen the suggestion that at this point the speaker is identified with Tiresias. However the nature of the mysterious woman, both sorceress, tutrix and sybil, is not yet clear and the clue comes in the last stanza where the speaker finds himself on the shores of light, the wisdom of the night fading, so that he is too dazzled by the dawn to read the scroll on which it is written like a palimpsest beneath another script.

The shores of light! Of course, the phrase is clearly an echo of the great invocation to Venus at the beginning of Lucretius's *De Rerum Natura*.

> quae quoniam rerum naturam sola gubernas
> nec sine te quicquam dias in luminis oras
> exoritur neque fit laetum nec amabile quicquam
> te sociam studeo scribendis versibus esse
> quos ego de rerum natura pangere conor.*

* 'Since you alone govern the nature of things, since without you nothing emerges into the shining shores of light (i.e. is born), nothing joyous or lovely is made, I desire you as my partner in writing the verses which I am trying to fashion concerning the Nature of things.'

Everything now falls into place. The poem is addressed to Venus, or rather to some beloved women who symbolises Venus. Through the magic and sorcery of the book of her body the scholar, at first bewildered, passes through the initiation of a series of nightmare visions and renouncing his faith by a pact with the dark powers of love becomes transformed to a poet and by the magic of poetry is able to interpret the mystery of things; then as the next stage of his initiation, reading the book of her body with his fingers, she becomes like the Venus of Lucretius, his partner in the translation of this secret knowledge into his own poetry and like Tiresias acquires the added gift of prophetic insight. Finally he emerges from darkness onto the 'shores of light', a common literary phrase in classical Latin for coming into the world, being born. There he finds that what he learned in the school of night quickly fades from consciousness and is lost, except as a dim memory, like the Dead Sea Scrolls in the Holy Land. But the scrolls remain and bear witness within. The poem, in fact, is a modern version of the initiation rites of ancient mystery religions; in this the lover passes through the steps and relives the myth to be reborn after the mystic experience of love. At this point our imaginary critic would almost certainly drag in Mozart's *Magic Flute*, which he would know to have been my favourite opera. And what about Jung?

But enough is enough.

This exercise in the style of the school of Henn and Melchiori has been great fun to do. I can see the fascination of this approach to poems, so that I now almost regret that I must destroy the scenario and the theory built on it and reject almost all of the supporting material. The title, 'The School of Night', was only added after the poem was written in its present form. As it was originally conceived it was called 'The Tigers have Eaten the Cage', a title I shall explain shortly. At the time I had not read Muriel Bradbrook's study of the Raleigh circle, though I knew about Marlowe's association with it. I also knew about the attribution of the phrase in *Love's Labour's Lost*. But I was almost completely ignorant of the play itself. If I had read it at all it was as a schoolboy and I had no memory of it at all. The idea of the body of the beloved as a sorcerer's book was indeed partly suggested by Marlowe's Dr Faustus but its original source was Donne's poem 'The Extasie',

> To 'our bodies turne wee then, that so
>   Weake men on love reveal'd may looke;
> Love's mysteries in soules do grow,
>   But yet the body is his booke.

There was no idea of an initiation or a mystery religion in my mind during the poem's composition and Tiresias was as absent from my thoughts as Professor Henn himself—what would he be doing in a love-poem, anyway?—As for the 'Shores of Light', I simply took them from the title of a book of essays by Edmund Wilson—essays for the most part on contemporary American writing. I did not know at the time that the phrase came from Lucretius and I only found out that it meant 'to be born, to come into the world' in the literary usage of Lucretius' day, some years later when I looked it up in my Latin dictionary.

The real story of the poem is more or less as follows. After ten or twelve years I have quite naturally forgotten some of the details of its growth, but because it was a poem which puzzled me I kept a few of the rough drafts which have helped in reconstructing the process.

Though the poem was mainly composed in 1967 and 1968, it began several years earlier, with a dream in which I found myself with a number of other people huddled in a large cage on a vast empty, bare plain at night. In a dim light that seemed like the first intimation of dawn or the last of dusk we could see various dangerous wild animals wandering round the cage obviously hopeful of preying on us. Suddenly the crowd in the cage began to break up and run about over the plain calling out 'The Tigers have eaten the cage'. In the dream I perceived that indeed the bars on the far side were no longer there. In the moment of panic I woke up and recognized the dream as a variant of a recurrent nightmare I have had ever since childhood, in which I am pursued by wild and savage animals, reach fences or climb trees, only to have my safety destroyed as the protection falls flat or crumbles away. The earliest dream of this sort I can remember is one in which the house was attacked by a lion and a tiger during the night and the family was forced to flee in the dark. I was about four years old at the time.

As I lay awake thinking of this chain of dreams, the idea
of a poem occurred to me, a poem which should be based on
some of these dream events. The original idea was of a sort
of ironic allegory of the Romantic movement, where the
cage was to represent the eighteenth century notion of rea-
son, which did not really control the passions as was im-
agined. The romantics, believing that 'the tygers of wrath
are wiser than the horses of instruction', had plunged us into
nightmare. It was not a very bright idea and I have little
taste for allegory in any case, but I made some notes and
returned to them from time to time, but got no further
ideas. At this stage the title of the poem was to have been
'The Tigers have Eaten the Cage'. At some time later I be-
gan to have an idea of a poem about love and making love
as opening doors of perception to a world of knowledge and
vision not to be explored in any other way. It could have
been described as a variation on the theme of Donne's 'The
Extasie'. Then the poem began to grow on its own, as poems
so often do. The body as a book became the body as a magic
book, this recalled Faustus and a poem I had written in 1964
in which Faustus finds that the magic book baffles his at-
tempts to use it, diminishes his knowledge and power
instead of increasing it. The initiate must go by another
road, the path of nightmare and trial by horror, from which
he emerges to solve the mysteries himself. I had got as far as
the third stanza when the poem stopped and refused to go
any further. It suddenly took off again in 1967 and rapidly
finished itself without my contributing anything more than
the reference to the Dead Sea Scrolls, which I had just been
reading about. I have never really known just what the poem
was about, but it got mixed up with the other poem about
the tigers and the cage because I borrowed the image of the
scholar writing in his own blood and the captives in the
cage from the earlier poem. Perhaps there were other links.
I would describe the final result as a sort of dream poem
composed in a waking state. It may be as incoherent as
dreams often are but it may have, deep down, an explicit
theme. Its composition began with the second stanza, the title
and the first stanza belong to a later expanded version. The
nightmares with which it begins are based on childish mem-
ories of seeing someone walking in their sleep, eyes open but

with only the whites visible, and whispering to themselves, on Goya's well known picture of the giant sitting on the horizon while the darkling plain in the foreground is full of fleeing humans and animals, on Fuseli's picture 'The Nightmare' with the sleeping girl on the bed, the imp squatting on her chest and the mad mare's head poking through the window. To these were joined memories of an account of vampire bats in South America, which I had read as a boy. I could go on tracing the images to their sources but I have said enough to suggest that my earlier account by my imaginary critic and commentator is simply wildly astray and that no matter how much a critic like Melchiori is able to dig up, there are likely to be unknown components in the poem, unknown irruptions and substitutions of ideas and images which make nonsense of his theories. And his theories tend to inflate and distort the poem.

It is one of the faults of criticism in our time: to analyse and dissect poems beyond what the text will bear. Earlier in this work I suggested that because of the inherent ambiguity and abstraction of language, there will always be *two* poems at least, the poet's and the reader's translation or re-forming of this original in terms of his own language habits and his own experience. One can go further than this: behind the poet's poem is the material from which it was made but which is as irrelevant to what it is in itself as are the soil and manure from which a rose is grown. This mass of artefacts and sources, this dung and dirt, is what Messrs Henn and Co try to add to the rose. On the other side, in the reader's poem, are all the associations and applications he makes of the poem he has reconstituted from the coded poem. These are perfectly legitimate ways of treating the poem. We may apply them to further reaches of our experience or our imagination, as long as we do not import these extensions into the poem. It is not always easy to decide in either case what is legitimate use of source material or of application beyond the poem. There is always an ambiguous frontier between the two. But the test is a simple one: Can you point to anything in the poem itself to justify your interpretation? If not it is irrelevant. It belongs not to literature but to biography, the biography of the poet, or the biography of his reader, and too often, I fear, merely to the biography of the critic himself. Too many critics of our day appear to me to use poems simply as raw material for an exquisite display of their own sensibilities. Even where they are not engaged in importing irrelevant material into the poem, they are exhausting its possibilities, they are leaving nothing for the reader's imagination, they anticipate all his possible discoveries, they forestall wonder and delight and the sense a good reader has of letting a poem reveal itself little by little. They advance on the garden of the Muses like a plague of locusts and leave nothing but bare stalks behind them. I have to say this not as an indictment but as a confession, since I have to bear my part in the blame.

It is time, however, to turn to a more general survey of the critical heresies of our time and their roots in the theories of the past hundred and fifty years.

II

Heresies of the Age

'In my father's house are many mansions.' John xiv-2

THE nineteenth and twentieth centuries have been extraordinarily rich in imperfect or false theories of poetry. These were usually based on conscious or unconscious analogies which were without substance in themselves and had a specious appeal because of the ignorance of poets and theorists alike of the real nature of language and the way it works in poetry. In fact we still know far too little about the *life* of language, though its structure and operation are now reasonably clear. We still know too little about language as a biological phenomenon, language considered as a living process of living beings, to be able to form more than a rudimentary theory of its most complex manifestation, poetry. We still think and talk too much about words as though they were counters, inanimate objects to be learned and manipulated. And this has been so with most theories of poetry up to the present day.

Unfortunately the limitations and short-comings of these theories were often concealed by the fact that in spite of their defects, poets of genius often made them work and hence gave them a spurious prestige. No matter how arid, mechanical or perverse a system may be, a poet with a real feeling for language can still make poetry with it even under crippling conditions such as those imposed by the elaborate crossword puzzle structure and the mechanical and forced double metaphor system of skaldic verse. The misfortune of course is that it takes a genius to make a silk purse from a sow's ear. The lesser talents are simply led into the wastelands, where they perish, still convinced that the master had given them an infallible talisman for poetry. Mallarmé will last forever, except for a few poems which are no more than literary curiosities in a museum which can exhibit specimens from nearly all of even the greatest poets. But the Symbolists in general are now for the most part museum pieces and nothing more. Most of those who have adhered to any of the later theories of poetry have in any case been condemned to making bricks without straw.

From Aristotle on to the end of the eighteenth century a single theory, understood in various ways, held the field; the theory that poetry was an art of imitation. 'Imitation' meant, on the whole, the imagining and representation in words, of situations in the world around and since in drama and narrative poetry Aristotle agreed that the poet could represent men in action as better than they actually are, or worse, or just as they are, this gave scope to myth and satire as well as to realistic presentations. A place could, one presumes, be found even for fantasy and fairy tale. This still leaves lyric poetry unprovided for and we do not know how the 'Master of those who know' proposed to solve this problem, since the latter part of the Poetics has been lost. But we can perhaps guess from an ingenious theory he advances in the *Politics* in the section devoted to the use of music in education. Since in Greece music and lyric poetry were closely associated and shared the same name, it is likely that he would have considered that they work in the same way. Now music, he says, is an art of imitation different from the other arts in that it arouses states of emotion in us which are 'imitations' of the same emotions as we experience them in daily life. We are in the same state of mind, but the cause of the emotion is the music, not a real object or an actual situation.

> Rhythm and melody, above all else, provide imitations of anger and calm, of courage and temperance and their contraries, as well as other spiritual affections which come very near to the affections themselves. . . .
> In musical compositions . . . there are clearly imitations of characters; for, to begin with, the musical modes differ essentially from one another, and those who hear them are differently affected by each. Some of them, e.g. the Mixolydian, make us sad and solemn; others, i.e. the softer varieties, enervate the mind; another, the Dorian, gives rise to a moderate

and settled state of mind; while the Phrygian inspires enthusiasm. . . . The same principles apply to rhythm: some induce restfulness, others excitement; and these last may be divided according as they are vulgar or the other way about.*

This looks like a rather desperate attempt, on Aristotle's part, to force music (and perhaps lyric poetry) into this imitation scheme for all the arts. It reminds me of the desperate systems of epicycles and other mathematical devices used in the later life of the Ptolemaic system to save the hypothesis that the sun and planets and fixed stars went round the earth as centre. But perhaps we simply do not know enough about Greek music—or about the relation of music to the emotions in general.

In any case during those twenty one centuries the 'Imitation Theory' was not much more than a comfortable intellectual cushion. Styles of poetry might alter but that was natural enough. It needed no theoretical justification. Whatever techniques might replace others in poetry it was still an imitative art. But its rival, the Inspiration Theory, also survived without seriously clashing with it. Of course the two *should* have clashed, since the first assumes that the poet is aware of the world around him and sets out to give an account of it, while the other assumes that his mind is taken over by an outside force and he does not know what he is doing. It suggests that poetry was not subject to much theorising, in any case, and that what theory there was, was technical rather than fundamentalist. People did not concern themselves with the question: what sort of thing is poetry? but rather with the question: What is the best or the proper way to go about writing a poem?

All this was changed with certain variations in practice and theory which occurred in various European countries in a period which we can roughly define as the last thirty years of the eighteenth century and the first thirty years of the nineteenth, when at various points within this period a 'romantic movement' took place. I am not concerned with Romanticism in itself, or with the vexed, and perhaps trivial, question of classicism *versus* romanticism, but with certain changes in attitude which the so-called romantic movements generated, which later generations inherited and which in-

* *Politics*, Book VIII, 1340 a and b.

fluenced their thinking about poetry long after the 'romantics' themselves had vanished from the scene.

The first of these changes of attitude, and perhaps the most damaging in the long run, is the view that the important thing in a poem is the 'emotion' it generates and that this emotion, which is the *raison d'être* of the poem, is an expression of the poet's own feelings and is valuable for what it reveals of his personality. Wordsworth put it very succinctly in the preface to the second edition of *Lyrical Ballads* (1800):

> . . . all good poetry is the spontaneous overflow of powerful feelings: and though this be true, Poems to which any value can be attached were never produced on any variety of subjects but by a man who, being possessed of more than usual organic sensibility had also thought long and deeply.

Although Wordsworth goes on to safeguard this statement with a description of how these feelings are to be modified by thought and directed back to subjects in the world around, 'so that the understanding of the Reader must necessarily be in some degree enlightened and his affections strengthened and purified', the basic change of attitude, which has continued to this day, was already there: The essence of poetry is the expression of emotion. The subjects of poetry, their presentation of a vision of the world without or within, becomes only a means to generate the emotion, or, as T. S. Eliot was later to put it, to find 'an objective correlative' for the transmission of the poet's state of heart and mind to his readers.

This attitude of mind obviously leads to the erosion and finally to the death of the Imitation Theory. The poet is only concerned with the world around him at one or more removes, not in and for itself, but for its power to generate feeling. Also implicit in this attitude of mind is a threat to all but lyric poetry. The great forms of the past are weakened and tend to disappear precisely because they concentrate attention on the world around in its own right. The impersonality of epic or tragedy, where the emotions of the author are of minor or of no importance, attract fewer readers when the emphasis is placed on self-revelation. What can we gather about Homer from the *first* two great poems of the

European tradition? The *last* two great narrative poems of Europe that were thoroughly alive and kicking in their own right were Pushkin's *Eugene Onegin* and Byron's *Don Juan*, both are sustained for their readers by the comments of their authors, the intrusion into the narrative of the creator's comment on his creation. By this means a personal, even a confessional, atmosphere was created in poems directed primarily to telling a story in objective terms and detached from their authors by the deliberate irony of their points of view.

So pervasive was this view: that the value of poetry lies in its power to arouse emotion in its readers, rather than anything it has to say or to be in itself, that Edgar Allan Poe in 'The Poetic Principle' (1848) could simply assume it as a self-evident truth in arguing against the possibility that an epic could be a poem at all:

> I need scarcely observe that a poem deserves its title only inasmuch as it excites, by elevating the soul. The value of the poem is in the ratio of this elevating excitement. But all excitements are, through a psychal necessity, transient. That degree of excitement which would entitle a poem to be so called at all, cannot be sustained throughout a composition of any great length. After the lapse of half an hour at the very utmost, it flags—fails—a revulsion ensues—and then the poem is, in effect, and in fact, no longer such.

Even granting Poe's assumption about what makes a poem, he seems a curiously weak vessel, if he could not sustain an emotion for more than half an hour. What of the 'three-hours traffic of the stage' or the excitement that will not let a reader put down a novel till he finds out how it all ends? What of the lover who can sustain the emotion of love, and in high excitement too, for months, even for years? Why is the emotion aroused by poetry bound to be so very transient? The claim that it is so is quite unsupported and is plainly absurd. What is to prevent even a reader afflicted with such easily exhausted emotional responses from laying the poem aside at intervals till he has recharged his batteries and so continuing to respond to the emotion and to sustain 'elevation of the soul' throughout his reading even of the longest poem? (Poe's attempts to answer such questions in 'The Philosophy of Composition' are feeble in the extreme and based on a puerile psychology.)

But Poe's identification of poetry with a certain kind of emotional excitement, an esthetic emotion aroused by beauty—is the basic confusion of his argument. This is the *effect* of the poem, not the poem itself. The poem is not a feeling, it is a structure of words designed, among other things, to arouse a certain state of feeling. We may be carried away by the exhilaration of a dance, but the dance is not the exhilaration, it is the movement of limbs, the rhythm, the whole physical activity, which produce the emotional state. The confounding of things with their causes is one of the simplest and commonest logical mistakes in psychology and, indeed, in all the sciences that have to do with the mind.

To return to Wordsworth's preface: he goes much further than his identification of poetry with the overflow of powerful feelings, organised by subsequent thought. He claims for these feelings a higher value, a superior moral and esthetic status, than other feelings because they are the feelings of a superior mind. The poet is a man

> endowed with more lively sensibility, more enthusiasm and tenderness, who has a greater knowledge of human nature, and a more comprehensive soul, than are supposed to be common among mankind;

Wordsworth could, I suppose, be right. Artists have to be special sorts of men, as well as specially skilled. It is the shift from the poem to the poet implicit in this claim that is the danger: the implication is that the poem is not to be valued simply in itself and for its own qualities, but for what it reveals to us about this rich and lively sensibility exhibited by the purveyor of these rare and cultivated passions which

> more nearly resemble the passions produced by real events, than anything which, from the motion of their own minds merely, other men are accustomed to feel in themselves.

Once this shift of emphasis is made the gate is left wide open to the herds of little confessional poems, the solemn revelations of the emotions of 'second-rate sensitive minds' which constitute so much of the admired poetry of today.

As a matter of fact there is reason to doubt whether poets are especially emotional, or exceptionally gifted in their emotional make-up, compared with their fellow men. I know a number of very gifted poets and they seem to me in their daily lives to be much like other people in their emotional gifts and reactions. It is a popular delusion that poets are very emotional people filled with powerful feelings which overflow in the passion and energy of their verses and that this passion and energy derive from the poet, not from the poem.

Moreover it is a dangerous delusion that diverts many young poets from the start into wasting their energies on simply expressing their own feelings. Poets, it is true, do deal very largely in emotion; they work in it as part of their material; they have to learn to represent and transmit what I have called the emotions *in* the poem and to master the construction or help the emergence of the structure and process we call the poem, which generates its own specific emotion, the emotion of the poem. For this reason it is important for them, in a sense, to be detached, *not* carried away by emotion, but to remain organizing, directing and controlling it. The delight of creation and invention is their proper emotion and this must be in control of all other feelings.

At the same time a poet is a man like other men, subject to the same experiences and feelings and these are, together with his observation of other people, the chief sources of his material. Emotion, in the first instance, can only be observed by being felt. Without the laboratory within, no poet can get to know and deal with this material. But it is only part of his material and only one of his necessary skills. The poem which is nothing more than an overflow of powerful feelings is one of the will-o'-the-wisps of the 'pure poetry' delusion about which I shall have more to say shortly.

I was, as I have said, largely brought up in romantic and Victorian tastes and attitudes of mind and unconsciously tended to treat poems as a sort of 'documents in the poet's biography', in spite of the fact that I was well aware that my own poems were hardly ever 'confessions' and were usually written in a spirit of 'as if' highly misleading to any unwary commentator or putative biographer. I was highly delighted once when the publication of a poem of mine, 'Morning Meditation', brought a shocked reproof from a fellow poet who had taken literally the fact that the poem was in the first person. Taken that way I seemed to be saying highly

K

scandalous things about the sex life of my father and grandfather. I contented myself with sending him Rimbaud's remark 'Je est un autre' to remind him that all poetry is not necessarily confessional. For all that I continued to read other poets in this sense till I was in my thirties. Even though I was also reading the poem in its own right, another part of my mind was busy extracting a *person* from it, the person of the poet. When I came to read the author's biography or his letters, or even met him, I was often taken by surprise to find a totally different personality from that unconsciously built up from the poems. I think I was finally shocked out of it by a passage in John Middleton Murry's *Keats and Shakespeare:*

> To know a work of literature is to know the soul of the man who created it, and who created it in order that his soul should be known. Knowledge of a work of literature which stops short of that may be profound . . . but it is not the real knowledge. The writer's soul is that which moves our souls.

I was shocked by this because I had never written a poem which had as its object revelation of my soul—I wasn't even very sure that I had one to reveal—I was shocked because I realized that so many contemporary poets were engaged in doing just this and had an adoring cannibal audience waiting for the next effusion of soul meat. I was shocked, above all, because I realized for the first time the force of Nietzsche's cynical remark that poets are the most shameless of men since they live by exploiting their own private and personal feelings. I thought of Homer, whom I did not know at first hand; I thought of those great and wonderful poems, the *Poema de Mio Cid*, the *Voluspa*, *Beowulf*, the *Chanson de Roland*, *The Saturday of Saint Dmitri* and *Sadko*, for example, which I did know at first hand, poems of the first rank and the highest genius, but of whose authors we know precisely nothing. I thought of Chaucer and Shakespeare, of whom we know next to nothing, and nothing that throws any light on their poems and for whom each generation of idolators constructs different personalities from their works, suspiciously coloured by those of the critics who had set out to reconstruct them. I am grateful to Murry, of whom I have otherwise no very high opinion, for loosing the scales from my eyes.

The view that poetry is primarily self-expression has been unfortunate in many ways. One of them is the support it lends to the destructive doctrine of Expressionism. I do not mean the German movement in the arts in the early years of this century to which the term was applied, but the esthetic theory which holds that, as it is the function of art to give expression to the artist's emotional life and vision, any means which satisfies him is a work of art. So to prefer one work of art to another is either meaningless (for only the artist can tell whether what he produces has given his impulses satisfactory expression), or else it is an attempt at *élitism*, a snobbish claim to superior taste and sensibility. Although this movement cannot be taken seriously and contains the germs of its own decay, since the trivial, the silly and the pathetically chaotic, the natural objects wrapped in cellophane, the collections of scrap and junk, the so-called 'concrete poetry' cannot engage the mind or the heart, or sustain more than a cursory interest, yet its sheer bulk and momentum in contemporary art, the loquacious cant passing for esthetic theory by which it is supported, insensibly influence serious artists and corrupt public taste. A sort of Gresham's Law operates in the realm of esthetic as well as monetary values. The young poet whose mind is tainted with the notion that if he feels he has 'expressed himself' he has written a poem, may be no more than pathetic, but he has damaged himself as well, he has cut himself off from that patient education in discrimination which the earlier chapters of this book showed to be necessary for the craftsman. Cut off from the providential interlocutor as well, he has become the victim of his own whims and fancies. Anything goes: there i nso objective criterion of judgement. He is as truly insane as the asylum patient who believes he is Napoleon or a poached egg.

He is in double danger because of the promotion and praise that the irrational now enjoys throughout the world. Here the German Expressionists, the Surrealists, the Existentialists, all the *aficionados* of the *mens insana in corpore sano* have to bear a great deal of the blame, though some of it has its roots far back in the implications and tendencies of various European Romantic movements.

Another sort of damage to poetry that arises from the 'Cult of Personality', to borrow a phrase from the vocabulary of politics, is the exaggerated esteem which novelty and 'originality' have enjoyed because of it. The poets of the past were not afraid to learn from one another, to imitate and adapt and build on a tradition which was continually renewing itself by this means. But, if the valuable thing about poetry is taken to be the unique personality of the poet, he must try to avoid anything that has been said or thought before; any style which is public or common—one thinks of the individual 'personal' styles of the great Victorian poets as opposed to the common public style of the eighteenth century—To be *avant-garde* is now a badge of merit, as everyone strives to be in the front rank of the stampede of the Gadarene swine to their destruction. The tradition, instead of continually enriching itself, is fractured and successively eroded and impoverished. Bad poetry, of course, carries its own death-warrant with it. The iniquity of oblivion does not always scatter her poppy blindly. It is the damage to good poetry that such false beliefs do by the way that is to be taken seriously. As I argued in dealing with the nature of language and the way in which poems come into being, a craft such as this which cannot be reduced to rules, of which no explicit technique can be passed on, depends very much on a continuity of *practice*. Break that continuity and it may take centuries for poets to rediscover the lost skills and habits. Break the links with the past and you have broken with the future too.

What was entailed in the shift from the poem and its emotion, the emotion generated by the subject and the treatment, to the poet and his emotions, was a new system of poetics. Byron, with his usual sound commonsense, perceived this and its probably disastrous consequences, in 1820.

> I am convinced, the more I think of it that *all* of us Scott, Southey, Wordsworth, Moore, Campbell, I — are . . . in the wrong, one as much as another; that we are upon a wrong revolutionary poetical system, or systems, not worth a damn in itself . . . and that the present and next generations will finally be of this opinion.

Looking back after a century and a half *I* am convinced that he was as right in this judgement as he was wrong in his judgement of posterity.

Still, the debate goes on and will, in time, be decided perhaps not by argument but by fact, the inevitable inanition and oblivion of the works written on the new system, and the continued vigour and vitality of those written on the old. I treasure a letter from the poet James McAuley on the difference between the two. This was in 1962 on the publication of my *Conversation with Calliope,* in which I had treated similar themes in verse.

> Surely this performance will drive the wedge deeper between those who embrace the new, and those who wish to renew the old, poetic. Basically I think the new says: a poem is *nothing more than* a record or equivalent of an individual state of mind with its tensions; and its 'logic of discourse' is *nothing more than* the correlation of its images with that interior state. Basically, I think the old says: that is true, incidentally, and as far as it goes—so long as you omit *nothing more than*; for in the first place a poem is the completed exploration of the whole world, or part of it, in a certain aspect (hence the function of celebrating and praising, which implies *seeing, grasping,* and abiding by an objective reality, physical and moral*). To treat 'the world' as functioning in poetry *only* in virtue of its capacity to furnish accidental correlatives of an individual interior state is a monstrous inversion.

When the time comes to stand up and be counted, I hope to be able to quote this succinct statement of what the whole debate is really about.

The heritage of the Romantics saddled the nineteenth and twentieth centuries with one other major confusion. It embraces a number of separate movements which I shall lump together under the title of the 'Pure Poetry' Delusion. It was a delusion that probably had more than one source. There was the old Inspiration Theory of the poet as a direct pipeline from a divinity speaking through him. Divine utterance was bound to be a purer thing than mortal speech. There was Wordsworth's conviction that the poet had higher sensibilities and more direct contact with the simpler, and therefore

---

* A reference to some lines in *Conversation with Calliope*:
  The task for which we grant the bays
  Is still to celebrate and praise.

purer, springs of emotion to be found in contact with Nature and in converse with humble and rustic people; and there was certainly the influence, as the nineteenth century got into its second half, of the theory of Evolution. It must apply, in general, not only to the origin of species and to the descent of man, but to all man's activities. Older forms of poetry were inherently likely to be the more primitive and mixed forms, from which purer and purer forms would be likely to emerge. The triumphs of experimental science also prompted analytic enquiry into the bases of all received beliefs. One of these received beliefs was that there was a 'natural' hierarchy of forms in poetry. At the top was either epic or verse tragedy and each of the descending forms was distinguished by its subject matter as descriptive poetry, religious poetry, love poetry, satire, meditative poetry, pastoral, epistolary or what have you. It was not a very satisfactory method of classification, since it was not based on any very clear system and the various species tended to overlap, but it had one virtue: it recognized that poems might be of different kinds as poems, and operate according to different 'rules'. The pure poetry movements clearly aimed at more rigorous and logical groupings and at defining the essential nature of poetry: poetry as it would appear when freed from all the other elements to be found in actual poems, poetry as it would be when it had evolved to its perfect form from the more primitive manifestations of it in the past.

Above all, the drift towards pure poetry, for at first it was not much more than that, was probably part of a growing feeling that the essence of poetry was to be found in the lyric, the poetry, above all, of 'self-expression'. It was also encouraged by the apparent decline in what until the end of the eighteenth century had been regarded as the two greatest poetic forms, epic and verse tragedy. The first was unable to compete with the new popular form of narrative, the novel, and the second was fighting an obviously losing battle with prose drama. A natural inference was that if fiction and drama could be done better in prose, they were not essential parts of poetry. There were even disturbing suggestions, such as that made by Thomas Love Peacock in *The Four Ages of Poetry* (1820) that poetry in general was an obsolete form of literature, belonging to primitive stages of society which modern social institutions had no place for. It was perhaps natural for the poets to retreat to the more defensible lyric and abandon the fields of narrative, drama and intellectual enquiry to prose. Certainly by the end of the nineteenth century poetry in these fields was becoming rarer and rarer and its popularity with ordinary readers was in decline. Practice was soon to develop a supporting theory. Reviewing Longfellow's *Ballads and other Poems* (1842) Edgar Allan Poe, somewhat defensively, stated a view which he believed to be novel and liable to invite attack:

> That our definition of poetry will necessarily exclude much of what, through a supine toleration, has been hitherto ranked as poetical, is a matter that affords us not even momentary concern. . . . We would reject, of course, all such matters as *Armstrong on Health*, a revolting production; Pope's *Essay on Man*, which may well be content with the title of an 'Essay in Rhyme'; *Hudibras* and other merely humorous pieces. . . . The observation is now recalled to corroborate what we have just said in respect to the vast effect or force of melody itself—an effect which could elevate into even momentary confusion with the highest efforts of mind, compositions such as are the greater number of satires or burlesques. . . .
>
> We have shown our ground of objection to the general *themes* of Professor Longfellow. In common with all who claim the sacred title of poet, he should limit his endeavours to the creation of novel moods of beauty, in form, in colour, in sound, in sentiment; for over all this wide range has the poetry of words dominion. To what the world terms *prose* may be safely and properly left all else. The artist who doubts of his thesis may always resolve his doubt by the single question—'might not this matter be as well or better handled in *prose?*' If it may, then it is no subject for the Muse.

It is a crude argument and Poe's abominable prose style does nothing to make it convincing. One has only to ask oneself whether the 'matter' of *Paradise Lost* or *King Lear*, or indeed of the *Essay on Man* could have been handled as well or better in prose to see that there is no answer to this question. You cannot separate the matter and the poetry in the way the question requires. As we have seen, each is indissolubly part of the other. A poem is not subject matter with verse superadded. If the question cannot be answered in respect of an actual poem already written, how can a writer answer it in advance?

But in any case Poe has already disposed of *Paradise Lost* and the *Essay on Man:* since they cannot be read at a sitting of not more than half-an-hour, they have lost their claim to be poems in any case. Now, in a single paragraph, he has disposed of satire and didactic or reflective poetry and we are left with what? Lyric poetry. (Longfellow's claim to be a poet rests on compositions like 'The Village Blacksmith', 'The Wreck of the Hesperus', and the 'Skeleton in Armour'.) Ridiculous as this appears to be it was a view that was slowly gaining ground. By 1880 Matthew Arnold, an incomparably better critic and a much more intelligent man than Poe, is found introducing *The English Poets* to readers with such narrowing views of what constitutes poetry as to allow him to deny the title of poet to Dryden and Pope altogether, and to refuse to allow that Chaucer was a poet of the first rank, because each of them lacked something called 'high serious-ness'. The frontiers of poetry were plainly shrinking in to-wards its lyric heartland.

I have paid more attention to Poe's essentially superficial and trivial theories than they would seem to deserve, be-cause unfortunately two of the greatest of nineteenth cen-tury French poets, Baudelaire and Mallarmé, became his devoted admirers, translated his brilliant stories and his mediocre poems into French and never ceased to praise and publicize him while they lived. It is extraordinary that these two minds, so original, acute and penetrating in their own criticism, should have been impressed by the specious sophis-try of Poe's essays. But it was so, and the drift towards pure poetry soon became a torrent, first in France and then in the rest of Europe. The Symbolists—like Paul Valéry, I do not believe there was ever a single Symbolist *movement**—tended to equate poetry with music, just as Walter Pater thought that all the arts had a tendency that way. Mallarmé did not go so far, indeed he spoke of the task of poetry as to 'take everything back from music', but his doctrine of evocation rather than statement, the view that to mention not the rose but 'absence of the rose' was the proper method of poetry,

* 'Existence du Symbolisme', *Oeuvres* de Paul Valery, Gallimard, 1950.

made explicit narration, for example, impossible and enclosed all treatments in such a fog of allusion and ambiguous reference as practically to amount to a pure poetry that made all the older forms of poetry impossible. In particular he banned narration and direct depiction in verse—with the dictum: *Point de reportage!*

The new attitude of mind which was rapidly becoming official doctrine is well expressed in Verlaine's 'Art Poétique' (1884).

> De la musique avant toute chose,
>   Et pour cela préfère l'Impair
>   Plus vague et plus soluble dans l'air,
> Sans rien en lui qui pèse ou qui pose.
> . . .
> Car nous voulons la Nuance encor,
>   Pas la Couleur, rien que la nuance!
>   Oh! la nuance seule fiance
> Le rêve au rêve et la flûte au cor!
>
> Fuis du plus loin la Pointe assassine,
>   L'Esprit cruel et le Rire impur,
>   Qui font pleurer les yeux de l'Azur,
> Et tout cet ail de basse cuisine!
>
> Prends l'Éloquence et tords-lun son cou;
>   Tu feras bien, en train d'énergie,
>   De rendre un peu la Rime assagie.
> Si l'on n'y veille, elle ira jusqu'ou?
> . . .
> Que ton vers soit la bonne aventure
>   Eparse au vent crispé du matin
>   Qui va fleurant la menthe et le thym . . .
> Et tout le reste est littérature.*

There it all is, the new Poetic, nothing but the music of verse matters, but it has to be a vague and atmospheric sort

---

* Music before all else and to that end prefers uneven metres, as vaguer and more readily melting into air, having nothing about them of weight or pressure. . . . For our desire is still Nuance. Not colour, nothing but nuance! Nuance alone weds dream with dream and the flute with the horn! Avoid murderous Wit as far as possible, cruel Brilliance and unclean Laughter, which cause the eyes of azure space to weep, and all this garlic of low cookery! Take Eloquence and wring her neck; You will do well in dealing with force to damp down Rhyme a little; if not watched, to what lengths will she not go? . . . Let your verse be a lucky chance scattered to the crisp morning wind which goes smelling of mint and thyme . . . and everything else is (only) literature.

of music. Nuance, the overtones of words rather than their direct meanings (*qui pèse ou qui pose*) is what counts for poetic effect. The play of wit and verbal brilliance is banished. Any hint of the comic mode is rejected. Eloquence, that is to say, resort to traditional forms or formulas, is forbidden and even rhyme is suspect—poetry has broken through into a new realm altogether, leaving literature, in the old sense of the word, behind, as a butterfly, or a cicada emerging from its pupal stage becomes a new sort of creature. And a new sort of creature it is indeed, moving among velleities and shadows, obeying that law laid down by the master symbolist Mallarmé: that nothing in poetry should ever be explicit or definite or mentioned crassly by name.

> Je pense qu'il faut qu'il n'y ait qu'allusions. . . . Les Parnassiens prennent la chose entièrement et la montrent; par là, ils manquent de mystère, ils retirent aux esprits cette joie delicieuse de croire qu'ils créent. Nommer un objet, c'est supprimer les trois quarts de la jouissance d'un poème, qui est faite du bonheur de la deviner peu à peu; le suggerer voila la rêve.*

It must have seemed a splendid and exciting manifesto at the time, opening gates to endless new vistas of poetry. Looked at a century later it is sad to reflect that those endless vistas turned out at best to be a narrowing road between high walls and at worst a mere blind alley. No one in 1884, by the way, seems to have noticed that Verlaine's poetic manifesto could have been a practical joke, since the poem breaks nearly every rule laid down for the new poetry. It does prefer *l'impair*, but is written throughout in nine syllable lines which are difficult to catch on to and, except for a couple of images, far from musical in their effect. It employs good bold slapping rhymes throughout, it indulges in rhetoric (personification), calls things boldly by their names, indulges in wit, even in a pun, 'la Pointe assassine', and in the impure and vulgar comic image of 'Prends l'Eloquence et tords-lui son cou' and, as for nuance, the delicacies of allu-

---

* I think there ought to be only *allusion*. . . . Parnassians take the whole thing and display it. By so doing, they lack mystery, they deprive the mind of the delightful satisfaction of believing that it is creating. The mention of an object by name, is to suppress three quarters of the enjoyment of a poem, which consists in the pleasure of divining (the meaning) little by little: to suggest it, in that lies the dream.

sion and adumbration of meaning, by a more than Mallarméan irony, it is suggested by its complete absence.

It is easy, of course, to make fun of a movement which nevertheless did produce some fine poems and led even in its failures to many new discoveries about the nature of language and the way it works in poetry. It is easy to forget, too, since it is now so far in the past, that it was a program for a poetry of the future. It had no intention of belittling the poetry of the past. Mallarmé himself was careful not to depreciate the achievements of the Parnassian poets; he had always a deep respect for their insistence on impeccable craftsmanship and limpid expression. Nevertheless, if one assumes that Verlaine's poem is true for poetry in general, it wipes out, by implication, most of the great poetry of the past, its eloquence, its clarity and colour, its miracles of form, its animation of convention and its unashamed declaration of the truths of life and even of the great truisms of human existence. The challenge to the poetry of the past is there, whether the authors of theories like symbolism intended it or not.

The same is true of such later attempts to formulate a theory of pure poetry as Imagism, which, having got rid of all the ingredients of the poetry of former times, including the mystique of Symbolism, proposes to make it out of images alone, and Surrealism, which makes a clean sweep of *all* conscious elements and manipulations and leaves it to the sub-conscious forces of the mind to produce poetry in its purest form. Even what appear to be such sterile and unworkable programs as the reduction of poetry to words treated as notes are in music (Gertrude Stein) or the lunatic fringe called Concrete Poetry, are not without some sort of rationale. Revolting and pointless as most 'concrete' poems are, they embody the play element so important in all poetry and one recalls that at least one major and important poetic tradition, the Chinese, depends for its effect almost as much on the pattern on the page and the beauty of the calligraphy as on the sense and rhythm of the actual verse. Even our own poetry depends to some extent on visual conventions. A well-loved poem may seem grotesque in reformed spelling.

There is nothing wrong in principal with these various

attempts to limit the elements from which poems are made, which the *ignis fatuus* of 'pure' poetry evokes. There is nothing wrong with the resolve of a painter, for example, who decides to avoid the effects of colour and to limit himself to an art such as etching. What is wrong with most inventors of 'theories of poetry' is that they want to deny all other practices as inferior or not permissible, and pure poetry theories are peculiarly liable to this sort of militant puritanism, because they believe their product to be the final and refined essence of something that other practices only achieve in adulterated combinations.

I have amused myself, from time to time, by imagining that the whole movement towards pure poetry in the last century and a half, besides the contributing causes I have mentioned earlier, may very well have been based on a simple mistaken analogy. The outstanding triumph of science in the earlier nineteenth century was the isolation of the chemical elements from their compounds, using the method of electrolysis. In 1808 Sir Humphrey Davy succeeded in producing pure potassium and pure sodium from soda and potash, which had previously been supposed to be 'elements' themselves. It was a beautiful and arresting demonstration and it was obvious that it laid the foundation for a sound theory of nature. It is possible that thinkers on poetry consciously or unconsciously hoped by eliminating all the ingredients of poems which occurred also in prose form, to find as a residue the pure essence of poetry.

A safer analogy, as I have already suggested, would have been the chemical bonding of elements such as oxygen and hydrogen, with poetry representing the resultant qualities of the molecules which are not possessed by either of the elements. They were probably unable to take this line because of a conviction that there is only one thing called poetry. But it may well be that there is no such thing as poetry in the abstract, only various sorts of poetries. Organic chemistry, though it made great strides in the nineteenth century did not achieve quite such progress as inorganic chemistry. Otherwise our theorists might well have taken a sounder analogy from it. There is, for example, a whole family of related organic molecules, some occurring in nature and some artificially synthesized in the laboratory, called the sugars. Their formulas, and the arrangement of their atoms, have a family likeness and they are characterized by varying sorts of sweetness, but they are all equally sugars and there is none that is the pure or archetypal sugar. Or take an animal group, let us say the coleoptera. There are some hundreds of thousands of species of beetle, all equally beetles: a specialist can give you a description and draw you a diagram of the ideal beetle, one that embodies all the common beetle characteristics, but it does not exist in nature: it is an abstraction only. This I believe is true with poetry. As a result of the combination of different structural devices, different rhythms and image-conventions, with different sorts of subject and treatment, each kind of poetry is 'a poetry' in its own right; pure poetry is an abstraction, not to be found in nature, nor produced in the study by refining away all the ingredients which exist independently in prose and there combine to produce other effects. You may, of course, prefer one poetry to another, as you may prefer honey to cane-sugar or saccharine, but you cannot deny the name of poetry to any of them. Each exists in its own right.

This is a principle that applies to all the arts. If only it was generally recognized we would all be saved a lot of pointless argument and half-baked theory. But the last things an enthusiast will part from are his prejudices.

But there is plenty of room for everyone. There are poetries to suit everyone's natural bent and there is no reason to suppose that we have discovered them all. It has always seemed to me one of the most exciting things about this, art that its resources are inexhaustible and that there may be as many poetries still over the horizon as we can see all around us. As Dryden said of Chaucer: 'Here is God's plenty!'

12

Ecology

ECOLOGY is the study of the interaction of living beings with their whole environment. In the last chapter I suggested some ways in which the practice and theory of poetry may be affected by its social or its intellectual environment. The interaction is mutual, since poetry affects social attitudes and values as well as responding to them. It is therefore convenient to talk about the ecology of poetry, though it might be more accurate to say, the ecology of poets. Poems are, after all, not independent beings capable of influencing and being influenced by their environment, they are things that poets and readers do, modes of action on and affected by the environment of these agents. But if we remember that we are speaking, not literally, but by an analogy with biological eco-systems, the comparison can be illuminating. We can in fact distinguish *two* systems, the specifically literary and the more generally social.

It is characteristic of ecological systems that the animals and plants which compose them have to adapt to background conditions of weather, climate, soil, latitude, elevation and so on which may be constant or variable, mild or severe. Within this setting the various populations of plants and animals are in competition with one another for food, shelter, living space, opportunity for breeding and maintenance. But if the system is reasonably stable they also depend on one another as well as compete. Some systems are relatively stable most of the time, in others the balance is precarious and often upset, while others are in open disorder and disarray in which whole species may disappear entirely or else the whole system breaks down and is replaced by another. Something very similar happens in the world of literary forms and among the arts in general. They

146

compete with one another and they form systems of mutual support. They have periods of comparative stability when, on the whole, mutual aid is predominant, and others of disruption and crisis, when rivalry may lead to the loss of a whole artistic species. The commonest form of the latter is when a new species of literature is introduced and captures the audience enjoyed by an already established form—an almost complete parallel to the introduction of the rabbit and the fox into Australia in the nineteenth century, which destroyed a number of native species.

An example in literature is the introduction of the novel in the seventeenth and early eighteenth centuries, which led to the almost complete extinction of the epic and, by the beginning of the twentieth century, of any form of long narrative poem. Another example, already noticed, is the demise of verse tragedy—except for Shakespeare—in the nineteenth century. Prose drama had captured the audience and verse drama dwindled and has now died. If anyone writes it any more it is mainly for readers, and few poets are tempted to attempt it seriously as drama. What they do is to write poems in dramatic form rather than productions for the stage.

Where animal and plant species have to compete for space and food, air, water and sunlight, poetry has to compete with other forms of literature, the other arts, and various other forms of 'entertainment', for the available time and attention of the human audience without which they soon dwindle and vanish. Most people spend much less time reading nowadays than they used to do a couple of generations ago, when things like television and reproduced music were not available for their leisure time. And on the whole what reading they do is less devoted to poetry. All this is bound to affect the sort of poetry that is written and the sort of public a poet can expect to interest. The general result, as far as my own experience goes, is that a poet today feels that his audience is a specialized and even to some extent a specialist one. He does not expect to reach the largest part of the reading public at all—those who read little apart from magazines and light fiction—but even among those with more educated and more definitely literary tastes, he expects the readers of poetry to be a restricted group, which one could compare with the devotees of, let us say, royal tennis among sportsmen, or of the harpsichord among musicians. Indeed, I have often had an uneasy feeling that poetry today has for most people a feeling of something surviving from the past, perhaps kept rather artificially alive by its use as a staple of education rather than by its acceptance as one of the fine arts. The enormous increase in the part played by English as an academic subject during the past century and a half—it ranks next to chemistry in the number of students enrolled in universities—may be more effective in keeping it alive than any appeal it has in itself. When, as I frequently have done in later years, I find myself at some public function, mostly at dinner, sitting between strangers mostly of the educated middle and professional classes, and we introduce ourselves and ask or volunteer information as to what we do for a living, if I say I am a university teacher my companions take it in their stride and ask further questions; but if, as I occasionally do for mischief, I say I am a poet they show an odd embarrassment and change the subject as soon as they can. If I had said I was a novelist, a dramatist, a writer of biography or travel books, they would have been eager for more details. These things have a recognized place in contemporary life—but a poet! What can one talk about to a poet? Poets are people, mostly dead, who wrote those pieces one had to 'do' for school examinations. Poets do not belong to the real world, even if this chap beside me seems normal enough. But he can't be: no normal person would confess to being a poet, any more than he would remark in a casual way: 'I'm a homosexual', 'I'm a forger', or 'I'm a psychopathic strangler'. To a certain extent, if I have interpreted their thoughts aright, they are correct. Poetry may once have been a profession like law, or drama, or novel writing, though I should prefer to call the first and the last two *vocations*—as professions one can have a career in the others, but not in poetry—not in our day. No one earns his living by poetry. The Muse protects her own by shielding them from financial success and the pressures from publishers and public that such success entails. Looking back at the money that my poetry has brought in over seventy years of work and comparing it with the rewards society bestows on a very average barrister or physician, or what I have earned as a critic of poetry, I repeat to myself a remark attributed to Alexander Blok when someone talked of a poet's career: 'Poets do not have careers: they have destinies.'

But if this is true of today it has not always been so in the past, or in other societies than ours. If poets in our society today are free to write as they will, because no one thinks it worthwhile to exploit them, or put pressure on them, because poetry is no longer an integral part of daily life, their own fellows make up for it. Poetry in the past fifty years or so has largely become a private and even a secretive affair; its language has tended to become increasingly complicated and obscure, as though to repel the vulgar crowd and protect the interests of the initiates. If society on the whole ignores them, they have, on the whole, retorted by cutting themselves off from society. Under pretext of being *avant-garde* and experimental, of enlarging the bounds of their art, they become more and more esoteric, cranky, and erratic. They move further and further out into the unreal. As an illustration of this I once took two passages from much larger works, one, the twenty-eighth section of Tennyson's *In Memoriam*, and the other a segment of John Berryman's long series entitled *Dream Poems*. The poems were written a little over a century and a half apart in time. Neither is a narrative poem, though a thread of narrative connection is in the background. In each case the poet comments and reflects on events arising from this narrative time sequence. In Tennyson's poem his concern is with the events and experiences of the years following the death of his closest friend Arthur Henry Hallam; in Berryman's with the life-story and death of an imaginary character called Henry who, like Tennyson in real life, is represented as grieving for the loss of a close friend. Each poem consists of a long series of short lyric reflections on aspects and events of a sequence which is not told in full. The extract I have chosen in each case refers to the arrival of Christmas as a sort of time-post in the implied narrative sequence. Berryman, who has recently died, enjoys a very high reputation in contemporary poetry, particularly in the United States. It is probably not unfair to match him with Tennyson's reputation in the English-speaking world of 1850. Here is Tennyson:

L

The time draws near the birth of Christ:
    The moon is hid; the night is still;
    The Christmas bells from hill to hill
Answer each other in the mist.

Four voices of four hamlets round,
    From far and near, on mead and moor,
    Swell out and fail, as if a door
Were shut between me and the sound:

Each voice four changes on the wind,
    That now dilate, and now decrease,
    Peace and goodwill, goodwill and peace,
Peace and goodwill, to all mankind.

This year I slept and woke with pain,
    I almost wished no more to wake,
    And that my hold on life would break
Before I heard those bells again:

But they my troubled spirit rule,
    For they controlled me when a boy;
    They bring me sorrow touched with joy,
The merry, merry bells of Yule.

Tennyson's poem is in a sense private and personal; but he speaks in a public language accessible to all readers of his day and even now containing no image, no reference and no word not perfectly clear and familiar to a reader of the poem, except perhaps the now obsolete word for Christmas, 'Yule'. Even so, the poem contains its own explanation for any intelligent reader. Here, now, is John Berryman's poem:

Christmas again, when you're supposed to be happiest.
The tree's decorated, the baby's agog with joy
& Santa is a white-thatched boy
down our main small chimney with his best.
I hope he makes, we had to have it swept
after one fierce day when flames leapt.
We must live alone; he did, it deepens.
Falling & burning soot is not pleasing:
we thought we'd lose the house,
Pride power loneliness, each in its season,
brought Henry up to three marriages
as up to Penn Station came Christian Gauss
there to drop dead, surround & alone
(Charmed swam the hero of the Hellespont)

as Gaudi on the street in Barcelona.
The fair lose more, having them more to lose
& the good & the geniuses.
Spent dangles of his life in colleges.
Then he limpt down the stairs & left the house

The general situation is easy enough to grasp, an American family Christmas, with a Christmas tree and a chimney down which the traditional Santa Claus is expected to make his way. Thinking of the chimney revives memories of when it caught fire and this in its turn leads the speaker in the poem to recall Henry and his three marriages, which the reader can easily pick up from the context of the work as a whole. So far, so good, Tennyson can rely on the Christmas season, the English countryside, to give his reader all the necessary clues. Berryman has provided similar clues in the main work. But here the likeness stops. Berryman is writing a private poem in a language of private reference. It is probably a poem which in its author's mind moves from point to point, coherently from start to finish. But the reader is expected to make the connections for himself—by guess and by God—We can follow these up to the point where the soot of the chimney takes fire and the family are afraid the house will burn down. Because the whole work is never very far from Henry, we are not surprised when he pops up by an unexplained private association, but thereafter it is *all* private association. What is the connection between Henry's three marriages and Christian Gauss (probably the well-known scholar of Princeton University where Berryman spent some time as a teacher) dropping dead at New York's Pennsylvania station? What is the relevance of this to the implied death in the same way of Antonio Gaudi y Cornet, the famous experimental architect of Barcelona in that city's streets? What again is the connection between these events and Leander (or possibly Byron) swimming the Hellespont—and so on? I have no doubt that the connections were all there in the author's mind, but he has broken the traditional contract with his reader, who is left to sniff the air and guess.

Confronted with such wilful solipsism, I have often found myself envying the poets of those ages and places where poetry was accepted as part of daily living and there was no sense of indulging in an abnormal, or even an unreal, activity in producing it.

In present day America and in much of the world beside, the poet feels no obligation to his reader. He believes either that he is a sort of dark oracle or that he has no contract to communicate. Such poetry may have its small circle of *aficionados*, enthralled by the intricacies of the sword play and the passes of the cloak rather than with the fate of the matador or the death of the bull, but this sort of specialization cuts them off from the rest of their world. They cannot complain if the rest of the world treats their poetry as a trivial game. I find the whole thing depressing because poets of great talent are rare enough and it is sad to see a man of real and exciting talent like Berryman, as his earlier poems revealed him to be, lost in such a blind labyrinth.

When, in Number 366 of *Dream Poems* he breaks out in defiance of such criticism: 'These songs are not meant to be understood, you understand. They are only meant to terrify and comfort,' anyone brought up in the old poetic can only accept the confession, but comparing it with what poetry has traditionally offered, he must regard it as a confession of impotence.

Under the older view of poetry and in many ages and different societies, a poet did not feel out of touch with his society. He had a recognized place in it and quite often he regarded himself as its spokesman. In the Scandinavian societies of the middle ages poetry was so important a part of life that a man like Egil Skallagrimson, who had fallen into the hands of his bitter enemy, the terrible chieftain Eric Blood-axe, was able to buy his life with a poem. Poets were an important political force and every king and chieftain sought their support in praise of his deeds and in satire on his enemies. It was the same in Ancient Arabia. Ibn Rashiq, a medieval writer, is recorded as saying:

> When a poet appeared in a family of the Arabs, the other tribes around would gather together in groups, playing upon lutes, as was their custom at weddings, and the men and the boys used to congratulate one another; because a poet was a defence of their honour, a weapon to parry insult to their good name and a means of keeping alive their glorious achievements and to ensure them everlasting fame. And they used to cele-

brate only three things—the birth of boy, the emergence of a poet and the foaling of a blood-mare.

In other societies, such as medieval Portugal under King Dinis, or in Spain under Alfonso the Wise, in Provence under William IX, Count of Poitou and the aristocratic troubadors, as in many a Renaissance court, poetry was an accomplishment expected of every gentleman and distinguished poets were honoured and rewarded.

After the Renaissance, though there are some exceptions, poets gradually ceased to have any public position, or to be the ornament of courts which they honoured by their presence. Goethe is about the last instance I can think of. by the end of the nineteenth century the break between poetry and the *res publica* was almost complete. The poets retired to private life and private themes and now continue to survive in their society but not to be of it, preserved by educational vested interests in much the same way that a threatened animal species, such as the bison or the Bengal tiger, is preserved in State parks and game reserves. Poets are living by literary grants and hand-outs in *their* reservations.

This is one side of the ecological picture. Another is a curious threat to poetry in our time which seems to come from the vast improvement in international communication. In the past a healthy and fertilizing regionalism prevailed in poetry, an unashamed provincialism, unashamed because poets wrote more or less for a local audience and changes in fashion spread slowly from the centres of culture. Today the unhappy demise of all the great forms of literature in poetry, has not only left us with what I once called a 'desert ecology' of small lyrics and private reflections, but literary fashions spread so fast and so readily from country to country that a sort of universal and deadly uniformity is setting in, even in the lyric mode. Looking through the magazines devoted to poetry in Europe and America, I am appalled by the emergence of what I could call the 'standardized poem'. It is in free verse, so that it has lost all claim to be lyric, but it remains largely in the lyric environment and in the ambience of the expression of personal feelings about private experiences often of the most trivial sort. Such poems have always been common, of course, but the alarming thing is that they

now seem to have occupied the whole field and that one cus-
tom prevails in almost every country in the world. I recently
attended a congress devoted to literature in English, held at
New Delhi, attended by poets from nearly every part of the
English-speaking world. They used to read their poems on
the lawns at lunch time. I read some of mine and they
seemed curiously old-fashioned and out of date among the
others, which were almost entirely variations on what I call
the 'international standard poem'.

I believe that the international standard poem, in Eng-
lish, is partly a by-product of the fact that in the last hun-
dred years English has moved from the position of a national
to that of an international language. It was Keats who, in
the fragment of his 'Ode to Maia', brought up the question,
at a time when the danger was not yet apparent or even sus-
pected. Referring to the poets of ancient Greece, particu-
larly those living on the islands—I suppose he had poets like
Sappho, Alcaeus, Anacreon, Simonides, and even Archilo-
chus in mind—he spoke of '. . . bards who died content on
pleasant sward, Leaving great verse unto a little clan.' From
what we have seen to be the nature of language and the way
it works in poetry, it is easy to see that the best fostering
ground for poetry is a society small enough and homogene-
ous enough in language and culture for the poet to be able
to rely on his audience catching every shade of meaning,
every implication and echo from the tradition and on their
sharing a common background of customs, religion, laws and
daily experience. Only under these conditions can words,
which are conventional signs and have no innate or natural
implications, attain not only their ordinary meanings but also
their full resonance, on which all poetry depends for its
richness of effect and its emotional charge. As the little clan
enlarges into a nation, and from a nation into an empire or
congeries of States sharing a common language, the poets
have to become more and more conscious that this language
means different things to the different sub-cultures that
make up the whole. Words tend to return to, and rely more
on, their dictionary and 'label' meanings, their rich over-
tones evoked from the 'clan as culture', the deep sharing of a
common way of life, become more and more etiolated, and
the task of the poet becomes more exacting. He is forced

ultimately towards a choice between a richer but limited provincialism and a thinner, more superficial, though more widely ranging internationalism.

The English language today is the medium of poetry for some two to three hundred million people in forty or more countries, including those in Asia and Africa, where it serves as a secondary literary language. The clan is not now little enough to comprehend so many cultures and traditions. In reading Australian poems to American or English audiences I have been surprised at the lack of real comprehension and response from literate and educated readers and lovers of poetry, not because they did not understand in a general way but because they missed overtones and implications of Australian life, Australian attitudes of mind, and Australian idiom. In the same way I once complained to the Ambassador for Ireland, himself a writer, of the difficulty I had with the language of James Joyce's *Finnigan's Wake*. 'Well', he said, 'there'd be no trouble at all, at all, if ye'd read it with an Irish accent'. He invited me to his house and read some of it with his beautiful Irish intonation, and soon I was following it with surprising ease.

I have often wondered about T. S. Eliot's claim that there had been a continuous decline in literary sensibility in English since the seventeenth century. I doubted it and I could see no good reason for it, but I have wondered whether there had not been a decline in the power of the language to spread itself thinner and thinner over so many cultures, with that vast expansion of England that began to get under way in that century.

The sort of problem involved is not really one of language, so much as one of background to the language which these untold readers share, actually with surprising ease. English, with its simple grammar of word-position and its uncomplicated word-structure, is an easy and viable world language—or it would be but for its devilish spelling. But as poetry goes, the old hen is simply trying to sit on too many eggs.

The diaspora of English poetry in recent times has been increased and intensified by such changes in literary education and tradition as tend to cut later generations off from the roots of the older tradition. School children who have to study poems of mine for examinations—God help them—often come to me, or write to me for help, because they find them difficult to understand. When we get to the root of the problem it is usually that the poems make passing reference to the Bible, or classical mythology, or other parts of the common store-house of ideas and images which when I was their age everyone took more or less for granted. What happens in one area of the diaspora, is even more pronounced between any two areas. *Alice in Wonderland* is unintelligible to the average child in the United States today unless her parents buy her a copy of the *Annotated Alice*, edited by Martin Gardner (1960). When I first encountered the book I thought it must be an over-elaborate joke. Who on earth would need scholarly and explicatory notes to a book so open and lucid? But it turns out in fact that most of the earth needs them.

I have sometimes wondered what an educated English-speaking Ceylonese brought up in traditional Buddhist religion and culture would have made of one of the most famous (and traditional) of the Olney hymns of Cowper:

> There is a fountain filled with blood
>   Drawn from Emmanuel's veins;
> And sinners plunged beneath the flood,
>   Lose all their guilty stains.

> The dying thief rejoiced to see
>   that fountain in his day;
> And there have I as vile as he,
>   Washed all my sins away.

He might know, indeed his English education might have assured that he knew, the tenets of the Christian religion and its symbolism. But could he, in view of his own and its horror of the shedding of blood, ever manage to enter into the spirit of that image of the fountain of blood in the first stanza? I find it difficult myself to take it literally, yet most Christians can, because they take it symbolically. This is a simple example of the problems that language is always running into in much more subtle and more important ways when its poetry has to cross too many frontiers.

Our English-speaking Buddhist might in time overcome his revulsion and learn to see, if not to feel, the poem from a Christian point of view. But with other poems he might find that he had laboriously to acquire knowledge and background information which a contemporary English reader would take for granted. By the time he has done so he is in danger of falling into the Henn-Melchiori trap, that of importing into the poem material that seriously distorts it. What was taken for granted, or meant as a casual or a shadowy implication, now appears as deliberate. What we were meant to infer from matters taken to be common knowledge from that knowledge into the poem, now becomes a deliberate reference from the poem to that body of knowledge. Instead of relying on the automatic working of the code-system which language essentially is, the process is reversed, the reader has consciously to build up and reconstruct the code, with a result that, as T. S. Eliot says of bad poets, he is conscious where he should be unconscious and unconscious where he should be sharply aware. The poem loses in depth, in resonance and richness. The language at this point is impoverished.

A slight illustration will perhaps bring this out more clearly. W. B. Yeats's little 'Fragment':

> Locke sank into a swoon;
> The Garden died;
> God took the spinning-jenny
> Out of his side.

To any literate member of the little clan for whom Yeats was writing, that is to say educated Englishmen and Irishmen with a basic knowledge of English history, literature and thought—I am trying to avoid the debased word 'culture', but I suppose that is what I really mean—this extremely witty and compressed poem is immediately accessible, in all its concentrated emotion, wit and implication. But to our poor Buddhist, indeed to most of my poor Australian students on whom I have tried it out, it is almost completely opaque. Asked to give an account of what the poem is about most of my students have come up with something like this: A man called Locke (some of them recall that he was a philosopher) fainted and some garden or other, probably Mr Locke's, died as a result (Why? It doesn't say, but that is what one would suppose from reading the poem) God took something called a spinning-jenny (a few of them remember Hargreaves's invention and Arkwright's exploitation of it in the eighteenth century) out of the side of his body. (What was it doing there? Search me!) (Why did God take it out in any case? How should I know? The poem doesn't say.) and so on. By the time I have referred them to the creation of Eve from Adam's rib and Eve's subsequent part in the fall of man and the expulsion from Paradise in the Book of Genesis; to Milton's view that this resulted in a general decline and decay in the whole of Nature; to Locke's empiricism, and particularly to Locke's separation of the primary qualities of shape and weight etc. etc. from the secondary qualities of light, colour, warmth and so on, so that the garden of nature becomes a mechanical physical world with unreal secondary qualities added; when I have reminded them of the new experimental sciences embedded in the new empiricism, which gave rise to the mechanical inventions of the end of the eighteenth century, which in turn brought in the Industrial Revolution; of Blake's attack on the results of industrialism, those dark satanic mills destroying England's green and pleasant land; of his laying the guilt for this at the feet of Newton and Locke; of Yeats' deep study of Blake and his detestation of Locke on other grounds; and so on and so forth. . . . By this time, as I say, the student, ignorant of all this background, has the material to interpret Yeats's four lines—but not the means of restoring the poem as a poem. He is in little better case than an illiterate who has first to learn the alphabet, then put the signs to the sounds, then turn these into words, then to combine the words and finally to evoke a poem. The poem has now become a poor thin structure concealed by all this scaffolding. Its most important character, its *immediacy*, its sense of spontaneous recognition, has been lost by the way. Anyone who reads the poem as it should be read must be able to take it in without having to think it out explicitly. He must feel, at once, for example, the contrast between Locke's morbid state, 'sank into a swoon', and Adam's natural though divinely-sent sleep. He must be able to pick up the overtone of the word 'swoon', suggesting an eclipse of the mind, as the eighteenth century so-called 'enlightenment'. He must be aware of the contrast between

Adam and Eve expelled from the Garden of Eden and the new Adam who kills the garden of nature, of imagination, and fouls and destroys his own nest. He must immediately seize on the play on feminine words in the 'spinning jenny' with its mechanical and inhuman associations (as the counterpart of 'jack' in *its* mechanical meanings) which contrasts with the fallible but thoroughly human Eve; and he must feel at the same time the irony of the creation of Eve from Adam's rib to be his help-mate, set against the mechanical withdrawal of the spinning machine from Locke, as of something simply taken out of a cupboard. In short he must be able to relive the poem, not to piece it together bit by bit.

This, of course, is what we do have to do with poems in other languages, or with a background of which we are ignorant, and we do have some success with such poems. But unless we know the language quite perfectly, we do not enter into them with anything like the success which a native speaker can achieve almost unconsciously. One effect of the enormous spread of English over so many countries and cultures is that each part is apt to read the poetry of the other parts as though it were a translation from a foreign language—diluted and enfeebled as all translation of poetry is bound to be. The result is a slow but steady erosion of the poetic resources of the language.

This erosion affects the poems of the past and those already written in the present. A small example is the effect of our recent change to the metric system. 'Kilometre' replaces 'mile' in our daily practical use of language and we soon accustom ourselves to the change. But few think of the effect on poetry and the damage to existing monuments of art. Already I find myself self-conscious about using the word 'mile' in a poem—yet the new word with its pedantic, scientific and technological echoes, its entire lack of the overtones evoked by the ordinary word, is impossible in most poetic contexts.

> How many kilometres to Babylon?
> Three score and ten.
> Can I get there by candlelight?
> Yes, and back again.

No it will not do! Even less will it do in such a context as 'whosoever shall compel thee to go a kilometre go with him twain.' Of course the language of these examples is rather archaic, so that the new word is the more incongruous. But it will not do in a contemporary poem either, say Robert Frost's 'Stopping by Woods on a Snowy Evening'.

> The woods are lovely, dark and deep.
> But I have promises to keep
> And kilometres to go before I sleep.
> And kilometres to go before I sleep.

No, a thousand times No!

The damage to language works in two ways. The useful, meaningful, old and at the same time contemporary word is uprooted and there is nothing to take its place for the purposes of poetry. But in addition the word so lost becomes 'literary' and then quaint and finally archaic, so that poems of the past in which it was used in a quite straightforward way, now acquire an old-world, perhaps a slightly precious, overtone which quite alters their effect—as though Frost had written self-consciously 'And leagues to go before I sleep'.

This is a tiny example of erosion and may seem not worth making a fuss about, but over the vast terrain of modern English, tiny examples occur every day, in every country and make cumulative changes as great as those made by a few centimetres of continental drift over vast periods of time. The language of the little clan is less subject to this sort of erosion because the group itself is small and cohesive enough to be aware of and resist it, or contain it within bounds.

The social forces acting on poetry, the relation of poetry to changes going on in society, is a fascinating and an endless subject of which we still know far too little. What we do know, however, is enough to banish nineteenth century claims that new forms of poetry were necessary because the old were threadbare and worn out. Language constantly renews itself and society constantly changing itself creates a new world in each generation for the renewed vitality of the old forms to deal with. For all this, there may be many new poetries, in the sense in which I have used the plural of the word, still to be discovered. Poetry does not evolve from primitive and simple forms to sophisticated and complex, but it does extend its range. The fears expressed by Vico and Thomas Love Peacock that poetry was a primitive form of literature produced by and dependent on barbarous societies in their evolution towards fully civilized states of man, has not been justified by observation. Poetry continually develops new metaphysical functions in relation to society. But that is a topic for my next chapter.

13

The Burden of the Mystery

> . . . that blessed mood
> In which the burthen of the mystery,
> In which the heavy and the weary weight
> Of all this unintelligible world
> Is lighten'd: that serene and blessed mood,
> In which the affections gently lead us on,
> Until, the breath of this corporeal frame,
> And even the motion of our human blood
> Almost suspended, we are laid asleep
> In body and become a living soul:
> While with an eye made quiet by the power
> Of harmony, and the deep power of joy
> We see into the life of things.

THIS passage from 'Lines written a few miles above Tintern Abbey' has always seemed to me the best expression I know of what poetry, the very heart and meaning of poetry, is all about. Although Wordsworth laboured for the rest of his life to enlarge and make this view explicit, the whole fourteen books of the final version of *The Prelude* take me no further into the subject and leave a less profound impression not only of what poetry does but of the truth of the statement actually released and embodied in poetry as it is in 'Tintern Abbey'.

Of course I relate it to my own experience and for this reason interpret or apply it in ways in which Wordsworth did not perhaps intend and might not have approved. The serenity, the sense of harmony, the deep power of joy which are necessary to the act of creation, the suspension of mind and body necessary to entering into the 'life of things'—Yes, that is the core of the matter. But I am not so sure of those affections 'gently leading on'. I have to interpret them in terms of emotions in which 'affection', in the amiable sense, has often no part at all; in my case it is often a fierce antici- pation, a wild surmise, an almost savage excitement that ushers in the idea of a poem. I am sure that when Words- worth spoke of the burthen of the mystery, of the weary and unintelligible world being lightened, he meant that the oppression, often depression, he felt in trying to understand the world was lifted from him in these moments of serene vision which lead to creation. I have never felt the mystery of the world, which is always with me, always growing the more intelligible as art and imagination and scientific research make it so, in the least oppressive. On the contrary, it seems to me a challenge, an adventure and perhaps the deepest of all pleasures. So I take these lines in a sense perhaps never intended by the poet. I take 'burden' in a double sense, first that of the 'gist of a matter', the 'essential contents' or 'weight' of an argument; second in the sense in which it has always been confused with 'bourdon', the bass or under-song to a melody, and with these I take 'lightened' in the sense of 'enlightened', 'illuminated'. Wordsworth, I am sure, would have assented to this as a possible secondary meaning of the lines.

I confess that this meaning of 'bourdon' has a special at- traction for me owing to a sense that has been with me all my life, that I can only describe as 'everything is set to music', as if the world as a process 'went to a tune' or an im- mense and all containing, continuing and directing rhythm. When I was a quite young child, I used to think I could actu- ally hear this melody or series of melodies accompanying the sweep and swing of time, and I remember, as I thought, sing- ing portions of it to myself. I sang, I didn't listen, any more than the instrument listens, but once an old clergyman who was staying with us asked me where I had learned that music and when I told him, said it was a pity I could not record it. Later the music of the great composers took its place, in the sense that to this day I never have any time alone with myself when I am not aware of a background, an undercurrent of music giving sense and direction to the sequences of living. So strong is this sense of living to music that I was more or less forced to confide the experience to a poem. But it seemed silly to do it in the first person since my knowledge of music is so slight. I compromised by attributing the whole experience to Vivaldi, in a poem entitled 'Vivaldi, Bird and Angel'. It is because of this constant impression that the world moves to music that I have never found the world 'unintelligible' in Wordsworth's sense, though it is sometimes bewildering, and sometimes terrifying. Set to its own tremendous music, it becomes intelligible by our participation in that music, in the sense in which Vico describes the *sapienza poetica* of the ancients:

> La mente umana non intenda cosa, della quale non abbia avuto alcun motivo . . . da' sensi, la quale allora usa l'intelletto quando da cosa che sente, raccoglie cosa che non cade sotto de' sensi; lo che propriamente a' latini vuol dir intelligere.*

We shall return to Vico in a moment. I have only dragged him in here for support for a personal confession. This sense of the Great Music, as I call it, I am well aware, may be no more than a freak of nature, a psychological oddity to which I am subject, as I am to hearing my name called aloud when I am completely alone—a symptom, I have been told, of some deranged minds. Perhaps it is simply one of those irrational stimulants which so many poets rely on, like Schiller's rotten apples. But I take it in the spirit of Negative Capability: It may be nonsense, but there may be something to it and in any case I have come to rely on it and it has never so far let me down. I do not exactly believe it, but I accept it.

There is nothing mysterious about poetry. The whole endeavour of this book is to show that it is composed of ordinary materials familiar to us in other contexts and that it works by similarly familiar processes. Poets are not magicians, but a rather odd kind of craftsmen, working in a living material which is part of themselves, by techniques of which they can give no very coherent account because the material, unlike that of most other arts, is not only alive but participating in the process on its own account. We still do not know very much about poetry, but what we do know does not suggest that it is not part of the natural order and

---

* . . . the mind of man does not comprehend anything towards which it has not first been prompted by the senses, and it then makes use of the intellect when, from what it senses, it extracts something which is not sensory at all; this is exactly what the old Romans meant by the word *intelligere*.

that the investigation of the natural order, which is man's great present adventure, will not, in time, provide natural explanations of most of the aspects of poetry which puzzle us today.

Poetry is not mysterious and yet it is a mystery. It is a mystery because it shares the still incredible mystery of conscious minds existing in an apparently mindless and for the most part an inanimate universe. Even in the biosphere, the tiny part of that universe in which we are in touch with other living creatures, poetry, in common with the other arts, is an apparent anomaly. Almost everything that our fellow creatures do that looks like creation for its own sake turns out to have a practical purpose. The dances and songs and mound building or ornamental structures of birds are nearly all connected with courting rituals or defence of territory. Man appears to be the only animal which creates works of art for their own sake and for the delight they give. Poetry may be put to practical purposes; a poet writing a love poem is practising a courtship ritual and Milton justifying the ways of God to men is putting poetry to the purposes of religious propaganda. But the poetry has to be effective in itself, simply as poetry or the application of it to practical ends will fail of its purpose. In spite of perverse attempts, like Tolstoy's *What is Art?*, to prove that all art is, or ought to be, in some way utilitarian in its origin and intention, the great works refuse to be contained within these narrow limits. They exhibit within themselves something unique in nature, the conscious self-moving, creative will, imagination existing in and for itself and free of all other purpose. This is a mystery in itself and in poetry this mystery becomes one of the principal concerns of the art. The mystery begins to investigate itself, strangest thing of all, for in this poetry is unique even among arts. Painters, composers, choreographers, may investigate the nature of painting, music or dance, but the works of art themselves do not—nor, of course, do many poems. They display what they are. Only in poetry, and in some of the greatest poems, do we get this spectacle of an art questioning its own nature.

Two famous attempts to treat poetry as a purely social phenomenon, produced in a certain stage of the development of societies and falling into decadence when that stage is

M

passed, are those of Giambattista Vico at the beginning of the eighteenth century and Thomas Love Peacock in the first quarter of the nineteenth. Peacock's *Four Ages of Poetry is* little more than a piece of literary kite-flying, whose main result was to stimulate Shelley to a reply in the *Defence of Poetry*. But Vico's views, neglected at first, proved very influential and in particular with Karl Marx led to the utilitarian view that the purpose and *raison d'être* of poetry was to serve the ends of the political ideology of the State, a view so well applied in Soviet Russia as to demonstrate its disastrous results in the 'official' poetry of the Soviet Union in the last half century.

Vico's view is well known: between the age of barbarism and that of full civilization, all societies pass through a heroic period in which poetry enshrines and promotes the knowledge, beliefs, and customs of the people in the form of myths, suited to the rude culture of the time. He paid particular attention to the language of poetry, holding that in the 'poetic age', what later ages regarded as mere ornament, metaphor and the related imagery of poetry, had at earlier times a quite different and deeper significance. Vivid pictorial images, comparisons, analogies and similes, personifications and symbolic myths were the means by which men were able to make sense of their experience of the world around them.

With the foundation of cities and more stable societies there began the emergence of real science, philosophy and rational rather than customary law. The medium for these was prose, and older religious poetic and philosophic (or rather mystical) theories which were rationalizations of social institutions, customs and practice, had to give way to these new forms. Poetry no longer had a function and it was bound to decay because, as Vico said, 'the order of ideas must follow the order of institutions'. In the last age of a society, the age of decadence and return to barbarism, men concentrated on pleasure for its own sake and poetry became no more than an over-sophisticated amusement.

Peacock's view is similar: in the first age of poetry, the heroic age, poets exist to sing the praises of warring chieftains and to belittle their enemies; in the second age, that of more settled civilizations and stable kingdoms, poetry still has as its function to support the ruling princes by praise of their ancestors; the third period of high civilization begins the decline of poetry, it diversifies itself in various kinds, lyric, comic, satiric, and didactic; it shows marvellous refinement. But sense begins to be sacrificed to sound and as prose takes over all serious intellectual pursuits, poetry is left with neither subject nor substance:

> Thus the empire of thought is withdrawn from poetry, as the empire of facts had been before. In respect of the latter, the poet of the age of iron celebrates the achievements of his contemporaries; the poet of the age of gold celebrates the heroes of the age of iron; the poet of the age of silver re-casts the poems of the age of gold. . . . Then comes the age of brass, which by rejecting the polish and learning of the age of silver, and taking the retrograde stride to the barbarisms and crude traditions of the age of iron, professes to return to nature and revive the age of gold. This is the second childhood of poetry.

Neither Vico nor Peacock, of course, had the slightest notion of what the poetry of primitive peoples was really like. Their description of the nature and function of poetry in heroic society was not unfair for the period when they wrote. But the record of man on earth goes back many millennia before the Greek and Germanic heroic ages on which they relied for evidence. *Homo sapiens* may have been on the earth for more than a hundred thousand years and, as long as he has had language, he has probably had poetry, dance, and song. No one, therefore, can say what the most primitive form of the art was like. We can only guess from the songs of contemporary primitive societies of hunters and gatherers who still inhabit the tundras, deserts, mountain fastnesses and great tropical forests of the world. The surprising thing is that most of them have a wide range of types of poetry. Songs relevant to practical occasions like hunting, birth and death, the initiation of the young, magic and the propitiation of spirits, the preservation of myths, and also occasional poems about ordinary events of everyday life and human relationships, purely personal expressions of feeling, are quite common, and so are what we would tend to call nature poems. In fact the range is very sophisticated and includes kinds of poems analogous to nearly all those recognized in our own society. Unfortunately for Vico and Peacock, the one

species of poetry missing is the heroic lays which they took
to be the basis of all poetry. As Sir Maurice Bowra observes:

> Primitive song hardly ever exalts individuals or any class of
> mythical heroes in the narrow sense. If it tells of ancestors, as it
> sometimes does, it is not to praise them for their courage or
> their sacrifices but to present them as examples of human
> behaviour, as prototypes of subsequent men, and tales of them
> are meant to explain rather than exalt.*

All this would hardly be worth noticing were it not that
Vico's views, filtered through later writers and supported
by feeling in the present age that poetry is an archaic form
of art, popular enough in itself but with no real relevance
to modern life, have become less a stated or explicitly-held
attitude today, than an ambient atmosphere.

One aspect of the arguments of both Vico and Peacock
seems to be well grounded. Nobody now goes to poetry to
learn anything about the world in which we live. Its function,
as stated and believed and practised from Aristotle to Dryden,
'to instruct and delight', has lost the leg called instruction.
Vico's long exposition in his second book, of how poetry was
once the repository of all the sciences, even of physics, geo-
graphy and economics would seem absurd today. This is
partly the fault of the poets themselves, who have simply
failed to keep up with the transformation of the whole uni-
verse which science has achieved in the last century, and who
have, on the whole, retired from public concerns to the
exploitation of private feelings. We do not go to the poets to
learn about the world we live in because they don't *know*
anything about it that we don't know ourselves.

But the other half of the story is that misunderstanding
of what poetry has to teach which led to all those rather
tedious eighteenth century attempts to rival the *Georgics*
of Virgil, versified accounts of Botany or of Medicine, or
do-it-yourself handbooks in verse on how to make cider or
raise sugar-cane. This was a false direction. Poetry cannot
compete in this way with science, or with any other depart-
ment of knowledge. What a poet *can* do, if he takes the
trouble to know the subject and respond to it, is to treat it
in such a way as to elicit its proper music, to make us feel the

* *Primitive Song*, 1962.

power and delight of what this knowledge adds to our concept of the world and of human life in it. But the poets of my time have been lazy and self-indulgent. They have not cared to know enough to feel the magic and the excitement of a world transforming itself. They have preferred to remain in the literary pinfold and to busy themselves with literary or personal problems more pleasing to themselves. It is perhaps just a matter of temperament that I have always found my happiest impulses to poetry outside these frontiers.

The whole question, however, has been taken from these unprofitable premises and set on the true one by W. B. Yeats in his essay on Synge. What we learn from poetry is not necessarily a matter of 'information' at all, it is an enlargement of our capacity to know. It is a freeing of our powers of vision from the way our ordinary occupations and interests tend to limit them and hedge them in, so that we can, in Wordsworth's phrase, 'see into the life of things'. This liberation does not mean that we leave the affairs and objects of the ordinary world for some neo-platonic empyrean. As Yeats points out:

> All art is the disengaging of a soul from place and history, its suspension in a beautiful or terrible light to await the Judgement. . . . It may show the crimes of Italy as Dante did, or Greek mythology like Keats, or Kerry and Galway villages, and so vividly that ever after I shall look at all with like eyes and yet I know that Cimo da Pistoia thought Dante unjust, that Keats knew no Greek, that country men and women are neither so lovable nor so lawless as 'mine author sang it to me'; that I have added to my being, not to my knowledge.

That is the gist of it. Yet he who can add to his being, if he has not added to his knowledge, has added to his power to know, to his range of vision.

I have a favourite image for this. Because I tend to think of poetry quite literally in terms of 'The Dance of Language', I was delighted, when I first came across it, by Karl von Frisch's discovery of the dance-language of bees, by which they indicate very precisely to the other bees in the hive the source, the distance and exact position of the flowers they have discovered on their morning flights. The dance, perhaps, has no esthetic interest for the audience, but it is a thing in itself apart from the message it conveys. I please myself with thinking of a poem as a thing in itself, a dance of language, and ideas, and feelings to be enjoyed in and for itself as it adds to our present being. But I like also to think of that other possibility: the explorer poet, like the explorer bee, bringing back to the hive a clue to unguessed flowery alps, new reaches of consciousness, new powers of vision, new honey for the hive.

This is something all the arts do as they too add to being, rather than to knowledge. It is what I call their metaphysical function in the adventure of man.

I once defined what I then saw as the main distinction between the arts of the novelist and the dramatist in prose and that of the poet, by saying that the former present man and human life in their psychological, social, and moral aspects, while the latter presents man and his whole world under their metaphysical aspects. I now think it impossible to make such a sharp distinction. Literary modes have no fixed frontiers or boundaries and often overlap. Yet the definition has for the most part proved true in practice even though we can produce no compelling reason why it should be so. When I talk about metaphysics I have in view attempts to present a whole, and if possible, a coherent picture of the universe and the whole world of man by putting together all that the various sciences and our other sources of information can tell us about their various special fields of knowledge, surveying what gaps seem to exist as yet unfilled and noting the discrepancies that appear between the various partial accounts from our various sources. It is of course an endless and an endlessly extending enquiry and like present day cosmology, cannot do much more than present incomplete and ambiguous models which further information is more than likely to prove false or inadequate, without itself ever being able to arrive at a final model. The reason for this may well be that the human mind and human reason are too limited for the task. It is amazing, in fact, that an animal equipped mainly for animal survival on this planet should have got anywhere near as far in its metaphysical quest as it has. As one of the foremost cosmologists of the day said in 1973 about the solution of the problem of alternative models of the universe:

. . . the relevant concepts may prove too complex for our minds to grasp. Progress would then have to await the evolution of a more intelligent species than ourselves.*

In the meantime metaphysics, in the sense in which I have used the word, has a hard job even to keep up with the new information and the new theories pouring in from every source. It is here that Vico's concept of poetry as an activity that, acting intuitively, precedes that of organized knowledge, adumbrates its formulations in poetic myths, and processes and expresses its intuitions in a form that its society can assimilate, may prove a valuable one. The mistake of both Vico and Peacock was to imagine that society would ever reach a stage at which it would be so rational and have so complete a view of the world that these services rendered by poetry in past ages would be unnecessary. Every advance of knowledge pushes us on to new frontiers, more exacting problems, confusions and conflicts, in which there is more than ever a need for intuitive formulations and poetic insight. We carry our barbarism with us. At the advancing edge we look out into mystery as much as '. . . the poor Indian, whose untutored mind sees God in clouds or hears him in the wind.' It was Shelley, in his unfinished reply to Peacock, who took up this point in the famous passage about the permanent place of poets in human society:

> Poets are the hierophants of an unapprehended inspiration; the mirrors of the gigantic shadows which futurity casts upon the present; the words which express what they apprehend not; the trumpets which sing to battle and feel not what they inspire; the influence which is moved not but moves. Poets are the unacknowledged legislators of the world.

So often quoted, so little regarded or taken seriously, even by poets, could we not perhaps take it quite literally? We will have to distinguish between what poets habitually do and what they would be capable of doing if they would take the burden of the mystery on their shoulders. But the immediate question that then arises is: Are poets bound to keep abreast of all that physical science reports? So many and such com-

* Martin Rees 'The Far Future' chapter 10 in *Cosmology Now* (ed) Laurie John, London, 1973, p. 160.

plex sciences—reports which in our age, are constantly re-
vised; all that the science of man and of animal life sur-
mises and constantly finds totally inadequate to describe the
fine structure and physiology of the map of living tissues?
The answer is, no, of course they are not! No human mind
could encompass the task, or join it to the other requirements,
the awareness of what religion and art, what the mere ex-
perience of living—with all its complexity and with all that
the ghosts which lean over our shoulders from the past have
to suggest and bring to the council table.

The proper rôle of poetry is, of course, to be what it is, to
follow the inner law of its involvement of the imagination
with the actual. But, in the wider sense which we are now
considering, its obligation is to take its place in what Michael
Oakshott has splendidly described as the 'Conversation of
Mankind', a conversation continually carried on by all the
institutions which represent not Science, not human en-
quiry alone but human art, human reflection on itself and
its means, human corporate organization and human indivi-
dualism, religion, the fine arts, politics and, perhaps above
all, the voice of daily living. These voices, sometimes assert-
ing themselves, sometimes dominating, often depressed or
suppressed for centuries at a time, always come to the sur-
face at length, because all are integral voices in the great con-
versation to which each contributes its part. Among these
Oakshott includes poetry. It is perhaps the part of poetry,
though he does not suggest this explicitly, to keep a watch-
ing brief in our age on the other voices. In another age it
may have, as Vico suggests, led the field; in an age to come it
may, when the other voices recognize its mediatory place, act
as their go-between and secretary of the whole colloquium.

Poets, at any rate in this age, which is all we can be asked
to answer for, are not called on to be polymaths, just to be
poets, to keep and tend the delicate, inexorably extending
edge of human awareness. As knowledge increases in range
and complexity, making more and more demands on human
abilities, consciousness must, in turn, continually extend its
scope and range, and this is the physical task of poetry and
the other arts, the task of 'adding to being'. A man who has
read the *Aeneid* or listened to the 'St Matthew Passion', has
passed through an experience which he could never have

initiated for himself, as he initiates, let us say, a week-end visit to a football match. The match adds to his pleasure and his knowledge of the game, but the poem or the music adds something to his experience of the world, unique and unpredictable. The same thing is true of all the sciences and all the arts, but poetry, sitting at the cross-roads of language, which all must use to communicate with all or any of the other members of the 'Great Conversation of Mankind', has a peculiar advantage for the secretarial position among them.

It would be foolish to pretend that all poetry, or that even most poems, have any metaphysical intent, or consciously set out to present a metaphysical view of their subject. There are, as I have said, many poetries and not all of them are concerned with ultimate things. But when they are, it is more often not what they say that makes them metaphysical, but what they *are*. The onlooker may have a clearer view of the dance as a whole, but the dancer, by entering in to it, comprehends it in quite another way, he has become the dance itself. He has not only added to his being, he has been translated to a being larger and other than himself. The difference between the spectator and the participant is that made by Samuel Johnson in distinguishing the effects of the sublime in poetry from those poems which, however fine in themselves, lack the quality of sublimity. The second, he says, produce in us 'rational admiration', the first 'sudden astonishment'. Something beyond all expectation or imagination takes us in its grip. We are enabled to grasp a view from Mount Moriah or even a peak in Darien. When we stand still in wonder at a new reach of experience which in itself is a challenge to the systems of belief and speculation in which we have been accustomed to live, or when these orders of ideas are suddenly illuminated, or given another or a deeper meaning from the vantage point of some extension of knowledge or a new range of vision, then the poetry which embodies this illumination, no matter what its subject, is properly speaking metaphysical. In one sense all good poetry is metaphysical in this sense and the simplest lyric, description or narrative in verse may be intensely metaphyical in its effect without putting forward any profound or philosophical view.

Any poet may do this without effort or intention, but it

must be said that the more he concerns himself with the meaning of the world as a whole the more readily will he exercise this power.

A man who has continually before him the vision of the world as a whole, the variety, complexity and mystery of the whole world of man, the sense of the past, the future and the present as one process, and the metaphysical questions that the whole world picture raises, a man continually obsessed with the passion for a synoptic view, cannot write the slightest of poems on the most particular of themes without reflecting this ruling passion, perhaps quite unconsciously—perhaps the better the less deliberately. It is this that gives poetry (which in itself is not either metaphysical or even reflective), its metaphysical force, its power of presenting things under the aspect of eternity—though eternity may never be mentioned. It is a light, itself unseen, by which one sees, the quality of love or hate, of comprehension or wonder, which implies all the rest.

There is much more that I could say, but this would be adventuring into a world of surmise and uncertainty. In this book I have tried to put down only those things I am reasonably certain of and have found to be reliable in my experience as a working poet. If it has any effect in suggesting a solution to critical problems and theories of our time, in promoting a clearer view of what poetry is and how it works, and above all in persuading poets themselves to be easy in their approach to poetry and adventurous in their methods, to keep in mind that theirs is one of many poetries and that such poetries do not conflict or compete, then I shall have done what I set out to do.

But the matter is not finished. It has hardly even begun. These are nothing and pretend to be nothing but a few rough workshop notes. I began by calling the book *The New Cratylus*, because, like the original *Cratylus*, it might pioneer better discussion of the nature of language. I am inclined to end it by calling it simply *Unfinished Business*, having in mind Paul Valéry's comment on people who try to contain the Word in a neat theory:

> J'en ai connu qui méditaient sans fin sur ce petit mot de sym-
> bole, auquel ils attribuaient une profondeur imaginaire, et

dont ils essayaient de préciser la mystérieuse résonance. Mais un mot est un gouffre sans fond.*

* I have known some who have meditated endlessly on this little word 'symbol', to which they attributed an imaginary depth of meaning and whose mysterious overtones they tried to define. But a word is a bottomless abyss.

Index